# *What the Big Island*
# LIKES TO EAT

# *What the Big Island* LIKES TO EAT

*Audrey Wilson*

Mutual Publishing

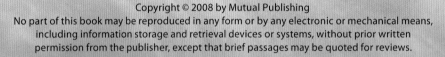

ISBN-10: 1-56647-886-3 / ISBN-13: 978-1-56647-886-1
Library of Congress Cataloging-in-Publication Data

Design by Nancy Watanabe
Full-page food photography by Kaz Tanabe
All other photographs by Jim Wilson unless otherwise noted
Cover photo: Wok Charred 'Ahi Over Slaw, courtesy of Merrimen's (see page 87)

First Printing, October 2008
Second Printing, April 2009

Mutual Publishing, LLC
1215 Center Street, Suite 210
Honolulu, Hawaii 96816
Ph: (808) 732-1709 / Fax: (808) 734-4094
Email: info@mutualpublishing.com
www.mutualpublishing.com

Printed in China

# CONTENTS

## ETHNIC POTPOURRI
### PLANTATION DAYS

## MELTING POT

## THE BIG ISLAND EATS OUT

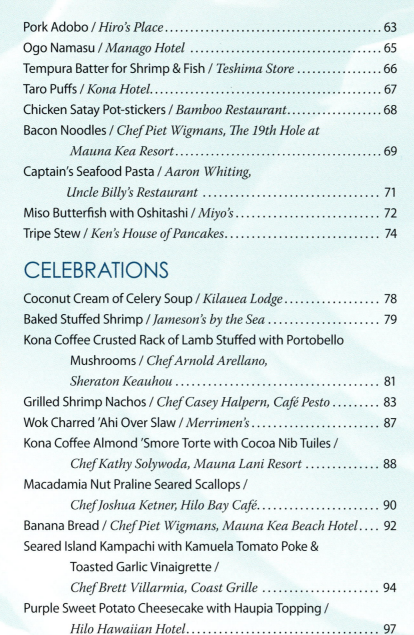

## CELEBRATIONS

# GONE BUT NOT FORGOTTEN

# HOMEGROWN
## FROM THE LAND

## BIG ISLAND OMIYAGE

## SUGARCANE SWEET

# INTRODUCTION

## ONE CAN'T HELP BEING IMPRESSED BY THE DIVERSITY OF CONTEMPORARY BIG ISLAND CUISINE.

But such diversity is hardly limited to the recipes in this book. It can also be found in the landscape, and among the delicious foods we grow and catch on our island.

We possess eleven of Hawai'i's thirteen climate zones, which allows us, as the biggest but least urbanized Hawaiian island, to grow a wide range of fruits and vegetables. These can be found in our back yards, at farmers' markets, and at supermarkets that buy from local farmers: sweet onions, kabocha pumpkins, spinach, guava, pineapple, papaya, just to name a few.

There's also a local fishing industry here, though many of us catch our own in some of the best fishing grounds in the Islands. We love fish and shellfish, and eat them raw, fried, steamed, and baked: 'ahi, mahimahi, ulua, moi, 'opihi, and many others.

Most of our poultry comes from the mainland now, frozen in little packages, but some of us still raise our own. Here on the Big Island we enjoy local dishes like chicken hekka—plantation food originally, but now a favorite picnic food—made with fresh local chicken. We also have the world's biggest ranch, the Parker Ranch, and raise our own beef.

Oh, and we also eat SPAM®. SPAM®, as you know, is canned, spiced ham. It's imported, but we've made it our own. (Hawai'i eats more SPAM® than any other U.S. state.) SPAM® became popular during World War II when it was the only meat available. We eat SPAM® for breakfast, with white rice and eggs; for lunch, as SPAM® musubi (rice ball with SPAM®); and for dinner, in soups and stir-fries.

## THAT'S LOCAL-KINE FOOD. BUT BIG ISLAND FOOD HAS ITS OWN SPECIAL LOCAL FLAVOR, AND WHAT MAKES IT SPECIAL IS THE UNIQUENESS OF THE ISLAND AND ITS RESOLUTE PEOPLE.

BIG ISLANDERS HAVE GRIT. We've survived tragic disasters: eruptions, earthquakes, and the tsunamis of 1946 and 1960. Many Hilo businesses were destroyed in the tsunamis and had to rebuild from scratch. Many of our food businesses—family farms, stores, hotels, and restaurants—have been operating since the early 1900s, passed down between generations like precious heirlooms. We have hardy survivors like the Manago Hotel (founded 1919), the Suisan Company (1907), and KTA Stores (1916). You've got to be doing something right to last that long.

An original recipe found behind some cabinets in Fujii Bakery, Hakalau.

In this book you will find all our favorites, reflecting the full range of our taste buds— Korean, Japanese, Chinese, Filipino, Hawaiian, Okinawan, Puerto Rican, Polynesian, American, European, Hawai'i regional, and Pacific Rim fusion. Food from all over, all mix up—reflecting the makeup of our people and cultures.

## THAT'S LOCAL STYLE. WE MIX 'EM UP, GIVE 'EM A LOCAL TWIST, AND ENJOY.

As for an answer to what Big Islanders like to eat—just give this book a try and let the recipes speak for themselves. When you do, you'll see why the way to a Big Islander's heart is through the palette.

# CHAPTER 1

# LOCAL GRINDS, BIG ISLAND STYLE

**OUR** melting pot of ethnicities has given us foods from many countries that we eat all the time. We mix 'em up and grind!

If you want to win an election, the way to amass votes on the Big Island is with food. Rice with Korean chicken, Filipino guisantes, Chinese sweet-sour spareribs, Portuguese sausage, and Hawaiian chicken long rice will certainly win votes if included on the buffet line.

Here are some of the tasty dishes that we eat on the Big Island.

# KOREAN CHICKEN MUSUBI

**MAKES 4 LARGE MUSUBI OR
8 MUSUBI HALVES**

4 pieces boneless, skinless
    chicken thighs
Cornstarch to coat chicken
Canola oil for frying

### SAUCE FOR CHICKEN
1 bunch green onions
¾ cup shoyu
¼ teaspoon crushed chili
    pepper
2 tablespoons sesame seeds
1½ tablespoons sesame oil
3 garlic cloves, minced
¼ cup catsup
½ cup sugar

### MUSUBI
4 cups hot cooked rice
4 sheets sushi nori or
    seaweed sheets, cut in half

*Musubi arrived in the Islands with Japanese immigrants who came to work on the plantations. The original musubi was a simple lunch food: a rice ball, which perhaps had a pickled plum inside. Hawai'i folk adapted this to local tastes, and the result was SPAM® musubi: a rectangle of rice topped with SPAM® and wrapped with crisp nori seaweed. Korean housewives took SPAM® musubi a step further, making their musubi with fried and seasoned chicken. This could be a complete meal if you added a green salad.*

**To make the chicken:** Pound the chicken to flatten it. Cut it into rectangles that will fit your rectangular musubi mold (which just happens to be the same shape as a SPAM® can).

Season the chicken rectangles with salt and pepper. Dredge them in the cornstarch, then fry until golden brown in oil that has been heated to 325°F.

Mix together the green onions, shoyu, pepper, sesame seeds, sesame oil, garlic, catsup, and sugar. Stir to dissolve the sugar. Dip the fried chicken in the sauce. When they are well-coated, lay them out on a plate and set them aside until you are ready to assemble the musubi.

**To make the musubi:** Lay one half-sheet of nori flat on your work surface, shiny side down. Center the rectangular musubi mold on the nori. Fill the mold with rice and then top the rice with one of the chicken rectangles. Press the rice and chicken firmly into the mold, then carefully remove the mold. Wrap the nori over chicken and seal the edges with a dab of water. Repeat until you have used up all the rice and chicken. Be sure to rinse the mold between musubi so that it doesn't get sticky. Let the musubi cool. You can then cut them in half on a slant.

# NORI CHICKEN

**MAKES APPROXIMATELY
12 STRIPS OF CHICKEN**

4 sheets of nori (crisp
    seaweed)
1 pound boneless, skinless
    chicken thighs
1 cup cornstarch

**SAUCE**
½ cup soy sauce
4 teaspoons sugar
2 teaspoons sake

*This crunchy chicken treat makes a great pūpū (appetizer) or picnic dish. Many Big Island okazu-yas (Hawaiian-style delicatessens) sell nori chicken. If you love it from the okazu-ya, why not try it at home?*

Slice the chicken into 1 x 2-inch pieces. Mix up the sauce. Marinate the chicken in the sauce for a minimum of one hour.

Cut the sheets of nori in half, then into ½-inch strips.

Dredge the marinated chicken pieces in cornstarch, then wrap a strip of nori around the middle of each piece. Deep fry the nori-wrapped chicken in hot, 350°F oil. Drain on paper towels.

# OVEN ROASTED KĀLUA PORK

**MAKES APPROXIMATELY
4 CUPS COOKED PORK**

6 pounds pork butt, scored
    at 2-inch intervals
2 tablespoons liquid smoke
3 tablespoons coarse salt
    (Hawaiian salt if possible;
    kosher salt will do)
14 ti leaves, stems removed
Heavy aluminum foil

The imu, or earth oven, is the traditional Hawaiian way to make kālua pig. An imu is a large pit filled with rocks. Imu-makers build a fire on top of the rocks; when the fire dies down, the rocks remain extremely hot. The cooks put a cleaned, leaf-wrapped whole pig (plus leaf-wrapped bundles of other tasty foods) on top of the rocks, cover the pit with leaves, burlap sacks, and loose dirt, then let the food roast and steam overnight. Imu-cooked pig—real kālua pork—is moist, smoky, tender, and delicious.

*Some Big Island folk still have imus in their back yards and cook pigs for special occasions, such as Christmas, weddings, and birthdays. The rest of us make kālua pork in our ovens. Here's a recipe used by many locals.*

Wash the ti leaves and arrange them in a circle, as a whorl of overlapping leaves. Put the scored pork butt in a large roasting pan and rub it all over with salt and liquid smoke. Then take the meat out of the pan and put it, fat side up, on the ti leaves. Fold the ti leaves over the pork butt so that it is completely covered; tie the bundle securely with string. Place the wrapped butt on a sheet of heavy aluminum foil and wrap the foil tightly around the pork and ti leaves. The foil must be sealed, with tightly rolled seams, so that no steam can escape.

Place the package in a shallow roasting pan and roast in a 450°F oven for one hour. Reduce heat to 400°F and bake four hours longer.

Kālua pork is usually served shredded.

# OMELET SHREDS

**MAKES APPROXIMATELY
1 CUP JULIENNED OMELET**

2 large eggs
½ teaspoon sugar
½ teaspoon salt
⅛ teaspoon black pepper
2 teaspoons water (or soy
    sauce)
½ + ½ teaspoon oil

*Several recipes in this book (including the somen recipe that follows) call for omelet shreds as an ingredient or garnish. Perhaps you know how to make them, but just in case you don't, here's a recipe.*

Beat the eggs, and add the seasonings and water.

Heat ½ teaspoon oil in an 8-inch skillet (a Japanese rectangular skillet would be ideal). Pour half the egg mixture into the pan. The omelet should only be ⅛-inch thick. Cook until there are no visible wet spots, then turn the omelet to cook the top. Remove the omelet from the pan.

Repeat with the rest of the oil and egg mixture.

When the two thin omelets have cooled, cut them into julienne matchsticks ⅛-inch wide.

# CHAR SIU

**MAKES APPROXIMATELY
4 CUPS COOKED PORK**

5 pounds pork butt or
    Boston butt, cut into
    1 x 2-inch strips
2 teaspoons salt
½ cup soy sauce
1 cup brown sugar
1 teaspoon Chinese five-
    spice
3 tablespoons hoisin sauce
½ teaspoon red food
    coloring (optional; but it
    won't LOOK like char siu
    without it)

*O'ahu folks can go to Honolulu Chinatown and buy fresh, ready-made char siu, or Chinese-style spiced pork. There's no Chinatown on the Big Island, so we have to make our own char siu. Here's a family-size recipe that you can make ahead of time, then freeze or vacuum-pack for later use.*

Mix all ingredients together and marinate overnight in a one-gallon re-sealable plastic bag. Hang the pork strips from the upper oven rack; you can use meat hooks (available at kitchen stores) or household string to secure the meat. Put a large pan underneath the pork strips to catch the drippings. Set the oven temperature to 300°F and bake the meat for one hour.

This char siu makes a tasty garnish in saimin, somen salad, or Chinese noodles. It's also the classical filling for char siu bau, or pork manapua.

# SOMEN SALAD

MAKES 4 MODERATE
SERVINGS

1 package (9 ounce) somen
    noodles

1 head iceberg lettuce,
    shredded, or
    approximately 4 cups
    shredded lettuce

1 tray kamaboko (6 ounce
    size), cut into matchsticks
    (julienned)

1 cup omelet shreds (see
    above)

1 cup julienned char siu

½ cup sliced green onions

1 teaspoon neutral-flavored
    oil for cooking the eggs

## DRESSING

2 tablespoons sesame seeds

2 tablespoons sugar

½ teaspoon salt

¼ cup canola oil

3 tablespoons rice vinegar

2 tablespoons soy sauce

*Did you eat somen salad growing up? I did. I loved it then and I love it now. Somen salad is a great dish to take to a picnic or potluck. It won't get soggy if you carry the salad and dressing in separate containers and mix them just before serving.*

Mix all the ingredients for the somen dressing. If you're going to be taking the somen salad to a picnic or potluck, it's convenient to make the sauce in the same jar or tub you'll be using to transport it. Put the lid on tight and shake.

Put the somen in a pretty serving dish (if you're serving it at home) or in the container you're taking to the party. Garnish the somen with the lettuce, kamaboko, eggs, char siu, and green onions. Pour the sauce over the salad just before serving.

# WINTER MELON WITH PORK

**MAKES 4 SERVINGS**

½ to ⅔ pounds lean sliced pork (chicken thighs can be substituted)

2 tablespoons vegetable oil

6 cups winter melon, peeled, seeds removed, cut into 1½-inch cubes (approximately ½ large melon)

1 cup chopped onion

8 large shiitake mushrooms, soaked in water and cut into strips

¼ cup oyster sauce

¼ cup soy sauce

1 package (.028 ounce) dried dashi-no-moto powder

¼ cup sugar

*Winter melon is a large squash also known as wax gourd, togan (Japanese), or dung-kwa (Cantonese). It was brought to the Islands by Chinese immigrants. If you don't want to grow it in your back yard, you can buy it at a farmers' market.*

Heat the oil in a large pot and sauté the pork with the chopped onion. When the pork is browned and the onions are translucent, add the rest of the ingredients and simmer until the winter melon is soft, or about 30 minutes. Just before serving, mix 1 tablespoon cornstarch with 2 tablespoons cold water in a small bowl; pour the cornstarch mixture into the pork and vegetables. Stir while the cornstarch thickens the gravy.

Good served over rice.

# EGG FOO YUNG

MAKES 6 SERVINGS

## EGG MIXTURE

6 large eggs

1 package (1 pound) chop
  suey vegetables

½ teaspoon salt

1 tablespoon sugar

2 tablespoons soy sauce

1½ tablespoons cornstarch
  dissolved in 1 tablespoon
  cold water

2 tablespoons oil

## SAUCE

1 cup SPAM®, chopped

2 tablespoons canola oil

2 tablespoons shoyu

1 tablespoon sugar

½ teaspoon salt

¼ cup water

2 tablespoons oyster sauce

2 tablespoons cornstarch
  dissolved in 1 tablespoon
  water

*Egg Foo Yung is a great, quick meal. Heading home from work? Don't know what to fix? You probably have eggs in the refrigerator, so all you need is a package of chop suey vegetables.*

**Egg Mixture:** Beat eggs well. Add the next five ingredients and carefully mix so eggs will penetrate the vegetables. Fry in hot oil, turn, and fry other side. Place on plate.

**Sauce:** Fry SPAM® in oil until brown. Add next five ingredients and cook until it boils. Add cornstarch mixture and cook until thickened. Pour sauce on egg foo yung. Serve hot.

# EASY MALASADAS

**MAKES ABOUT 60 MALASADAS**

7 cups flour

4½ teaspoons active dry yeast

1 teaspoon sugar

½ cup warm (100 degree) water

1 teaspoon salt

½ cup sugar

7 large eggs, well beaten

¼ cup melted butter

1 (12 ounce) can evaporated milk

1 can water from milk can

1 teaspoon lemon extract

Canola oil for deep drying

1 cup sugar

½ teaspoon ground cinnamon

*Malasadas are fluffy, round, sweet Portuguese donuts. You can buy them all over the island. My favorite malasada places are Tex Drive In in Honokaa, Punalu'u Bake Shop in Pahala, and Kawamoto Vegetable Store in Hilo (Wednesday only). You can also make them at home.*

*These easy malasadas are mixed the previous evening and allowed to rise overnight. In the early morning, just heat your frying oil to 375°F, fry your donuts, and enjoy them with your morning coffee.*

In a small bowl, mix the yeast, the I teaspoon of sugar, and the warm water. Let stand 5 minutes. Sift together flour, salt and ½ cup sugar into a large bowl. Make a well and add eggs, butter, milk and milk water, lemon extract, and yeast mixture. Beat together to form a soft, smooth dough. Cover and refrigerate overnight.

Heat your frying oil to 375°F. Pull a ball of dough approximately ⅛ cup in size from the mass of dough. (If you have a spoon or scoop of the right size, you can use that; less mess.) Poke a finger in the middle of the ball of dough, then drop the dough into the hot oil. Don't crowd the oil. When the malasadas are nicely browned, remove them from the oil and drain briefly on paper towels before serving.

Why poke your finger into the dough? This ensures that even the center of the dough ball cooks. Your malasadas might be slightly lopsided, but they won't have gooey, under-cooked centers.

# SWEET-SOUR LEMONS

**MAKES 1 GALLON LEMONS**

3 pounds lemons
1 cup Hawaiian salt
2 cups brown sugar
1 teaspoon Chinese five-
  spice
1 (1-gallon) jar (we used old
  mayonnaise jars)

*In the old days, many Big Island folks with a lemon tree in their yards would make preserved lemons. Not Moroccan-style preserved lemons, but local-kine lemons with sugar and Chinese five-spice. They're good for a sore throat or just plain snacking.*

Wash and scrub the lemons. Pack tightly in a gallon jar. Add 1 cup Hawaiian salt. Dry in the sun for one month. Top of the roof is good.

Take out the lemons and throw away the water in the jar. Cut the lemons in half and take out the seeds. Fill the cavities of the lemons with 1 heaping mixture of brown sugar and Chinese five-spice. Dry for 15 days.

Again, take out the lemons and throw away the liquid in the jar. Mix together 2 teaspoons Chinese five-spice and 2 cups brown sugar. Put 1½ teaspoons of the sugar and five-spice mixture into the lemons. Carefully pack the lemons into the jar and put it back out in the sun. Dry for 15 days.

After the last 15 days of drying in the sun, the sweet-sour lemons can be stored in a covered container in the cupboard or on the kitchen counter.

# ICE CAKE

**MAKES 6 ICE CAKES**

1 cup water
1 tablespoon sugar
¼ cup strawberry syrup
¼ cup evaporated milk
6 pleated paper cups

*Mom-and-pop stores used to sell ice cakes frozen in pleated paper cups, the kind used with water dispensers. Ice cakes were cheap and oh so 'ono on a hot day.*

Mix the water and sugar in a heavy pot and bring to a boil over medium heat; cook until the sugar is dissolved. Cool the sugar syrup.

Mix the sugar syrup, strawberry syrup, and the evaporated milk. Pour the mixture into the pleated paper cups, or into the pukas of an ice tray. Freeze.

# GOODIE SHERBET

**MAKES 10 TO 12 SERVINGS**

1 (12 ounce can) strawberry
    soda
2 (12 ounce cans) lemon-lime
    soda
1 (14 ounce) can sweetened
    condensed milk
1¾ cups milk
10 to 12 foam or paper
    disposable beverage cups
    (4 ounce size)

*Here's another local frozen treat. This one doesn't even require cooking!*

(If you don't want to use disposable cups, try making this in ice cube trays.)

Combine sodas, condensed milk, and milk in a large bowl. Mix the ingredients slowly and carefully (too much elbow action and the sherbet will lose its fizz). Pour the mixture into the beverage cups; fill each cup only half full. The sherbet will expand as it freezes. Freeze the cups overnight and serve frozen.

Maku'u Farmers Market on
a typical Sunday morning.

# CHAPTER 2

# ETHNIC POTPOURRI: PLANTATION DAYS

In the middle and late nineteenth century, after many failed attempts, Hawaiian sugar planters learned how to grow and sell sugar at a profit. Sugar plantations were started all over the Islands, thirteen on the Big Island alone. Plantation owners wanted cheap labor and looked overseas to find it. They imported indentured laborers from China, then Japan, Madeira and the Azores, Puerto Rico, Okinawa, Korea, and the Philippines.

Most of these immigrants hoped to work for a couple of years and return home wealthy. They were often disappointed. They toiled long hours in the fields, in the hot sun or drenching rains, for little pay.

Some came with their families. Many came as single men, and later imported brides. Plantation owners settled the workers and their families in dormitories or shacks, segregated by ethnicity and language. There were Japanese camps, Portuguese camps, Filipino camps, and so on. Each camp cultivated familiar plants and ate familiar cuisine. Japanese housewives grew and pickled daikon; Korean housewives made kim chee; Portuguese housewives baked bread.

But segregation couldn't last. Immigrants shared lunch buckets and bentos, intermarried, and traded recipes. Today these mixtures are all called "local." We still remember the bright spots from the plantation days, the good times and good food. Many of us still make cherished recipes inherited from our hard-working tūtū. Here are a few.

An old lunch pail used by a typical plantation worker. This one has a number painted on the top so the owner could quickly identify his lunch can or "bento-bako." Photo courtesy of Alan Kelii.

# SWEET AND SOUR SPARERIBS

**MAKES 6 SERVINGS**

1 pound spareribs

1½ tablespoons soy sauce

1 tablespoon + ½ cup brown sugar

1½ tablespoons cornstarch

1 tablespoon canola oil

4 cloves garlic, chopped coarsely

4 (½-inch) slices of ginger

⅓ cup white vinegar

½ cup water

## CHINESE CAMP

The Chinese came early to the Islands. A few Chinese sailors accompanied Captain Cook in 1778, and the first Chinese indentured laborers were imported in 1852. These immigrants were single men who often married Hawaiian women. Others brought wives from China. They left the plantations, started stores and farms of their own, and prospered. Chinese food, bought from the itinerant manapua man or consumed at an inexpensive Chinese restaurant, became popular with all ethnic groups.

*Sweet and sour spareribs is a favorite Chinese dish. These spareribs are marinated overnight so that the meat is infused with the sweet tang of soy sauce and sugar.*

*I like my ribs with daikon and carrot pickle. The tart vegetables complement the sweet meat.*

Make the marinade by mixing the soy sauce, 1 tablespoon of the brown sugar, and the cornstarch. Put the spareribs into a 1-gallon size re-sealable plastic bag and pour the marinade over the ribs. Seal the bag and leave it in the refrigerator overnight. Turn the bag a couple of times to make sure that all the meat is evenly marinated.

The next day, heat the canola oil in a medium sized stew pot over a brisk heat. When it's hot, add the marinated ribs. Keep turning them so that they brown on all sides. The cornstarch from the marinade may stick to the bottom of the pan; don't worry about it, just scrape it up with a spatula before it hardens. The cornstarch will thicken the sauce later. When the ribs are brown, add the garlic and ginger and sauté for a few more minutes.

Add the vinegar, water, and the rest of the brown sugar. Cook on low heat for 1½ hours, until the spareribs are soft and the sauce is thick.

# DAIKON AND CARROT PICKLE

**MAKES 6 SERVINGS**

1 (7 inch long) daikon, peeled
2 medium carrots, peeled
2 teaspoons salt
2 teaspoons sugar

*Many Asian cultures eat pickled vegetables, the Chinese among them. You won't get this sort of relish at many Chinese restaurants, but you'll find it on family dinner tables.*

Slice the daikon and carrots crosswise, in thin round sections, as thin as you can slice them. Put the slices in a bowl, add the sugar and salt, and mix to combine. Let the relish stand at room temperature for at least twohours. Squeeze out the water, and serve.

# SEKIHAN

MAKES 6 TO 8 SERVINGS

2 cups sweet mochi rice

½ cup regular short grain rice

½ cup azuki beans

Reserved cooking water from beans, plus plain water, to make 2½ cups liquid

2 drops red food coloring

Salt to taste

2 tablespoons goma (toasted sesame seeds)

1 (1.4 ounce) package shiofuku kombu (dried salted seaweed)

*Sekihan is often served with a sesame seed and shiofuku kombu garnish scattered over the top.*

## JAPANESE CAMP

The first Japanese came to Hawai'i in 1868 to work in the sugar fields. They brought their religions, traditions, and cuisine, and handed them down from generation to generation.

*One tradition is still widely observed: whenever there is a celebration, whether it is the birth of a child, a birthday, a wedding, an anniversary, or a holiday, you must serve sekihan, or red rice. Sekihan symbolizes good health and prosperity.*

Rinse the beans, then put in a large pot and add enough water to cover the beans. Bring to a boil, skim off any foam, then turn off the heat and put a lid on the pot. Soak the beans for at least 2 hours; overnight is better. Drain and rinse the beans, put them back in the pot, and cover with water again. Cook the beans over medium heat for 40 minutes. Remove them from heat and let them stand for 30 minutes. Check the beans to make sure they are soft. If they aren't, cook them another 15 minutes or so, until they are soft but not mushy. Drain the beans and save the water in which they cooked.

Put the bean water into a large measuring cup (4-cup size, if you have one). Do you have 2½ cups bean water? If not, add plain water until you have 2½ cups liquid. If you have too much bean water, pour some of it off. You need the 2½ cups liquid to cook the rice.

Measure out the rice (both varieties) into your rice-cooking pot or rice cooker bowl. You're going to cook them together. Rinse the mixed rice, then add the 2½ cups bean water and the cooked beans. Tint with 2 drops of red food coloring. Gently mix the rice and beans (don't mush them together; the beans should remain separate). Let the rice and beans stand at room temperature for 30 minutes. Then cook the sekihan in your rice cooker or rice pot. The sekihan is done when all the water is absorbed and the rice is soft. The beans tend to float to the top during cooking, so you will probably have to gently mix the rice and beans again. Salt to taste.

# AKU BURGERS

**MAKES 12 BURGERS**

1 pound aku (all bones
    removed, chopped)
1½ teaspoons salt
2 tablespoons sugar
½ cup finely chopped onions
½ cup slivered gobo
    (burdock)
1 large egg

Many Japanese plantation workers left the plantations to start their own businesses—sometimes in rural areas, sometimes in the larger towns. Hilo, the largest town on the Big Island, had its own Japan-town, known as Shinmachi (New Town). Shinmachi, alas, was totally destroyed in the 1946 tsunami, which killed 159 people throughout the Islands and 96 in Hilo alone—many of them were from Shinmachi, which was exposed to the full force of the enormous waves. Today, that land is a public park.

*Hilo has always been home to many fishermen. In the old days, fishermen got the best price for 'ahi, the large bigeye or yellowfin tuna. When they caught aku, the small skipjack tuna, they gave them away. Thrifty Shinmachi residents used to make burgers from aku. This recipe was handed down from those living in Shinmachi from 1920-1946.*

Chop the fish until it is the consistency of ground meat. Add the salt, sugar, onions, and gobo, and continue to chop until all ingredients are mixed together and are finely chopped. Add egg, mix well.

Add enough canola oil to a frying pan to coat the bottom. Make one patty, approximately ½-inch thick and 2 inches in diameter. Fry one, taste. Add salt or sugar to adjust flavors, then make up the rest of the patties. Fry the patties and drain on a paper towel before serving.

# PORTUGUESE WHITE BREAD

**MAKES 8 SANDWICH LOAVES**

2 packages (approximately
   2 tablespoons) dry yeast

1½ cups lukewarm water for
   yeast (100°F)

1 teaspoon sugar

5 pounds (approximately
   20 cups) all-purpose white
   flour or white bread flour

1 cup sugar

1 tablespoon salt

1½ cups melted shortening

4½ cups water

## PORTUGUESE CAMP

There have been Portuguese living in the Islands ever since the first Portuguese sailor jumped ship in the late eighteenth century. However, the Portuguese community was small, only a few dozen at most, until the sugar plantations started to import laborers from the Portuguese-owned, mid-Atlantic islands of Madeira and the Azores. Large Portuguese migrations began in 1878 and continued for several decades.

Hawai'i's Portuguese community has had a big influence on the food we eat now. They contributed the ever-popular Portuguese sausage, Portuguese bean soup, vinha d'alhos, sweet bread, and malasadas to Hawai'i cuisine. They also contributed the 'ukulele, but "no can eat 'ukulele."

The Portuguese Chamber of Commerce holds an annual "Portuguese Day in the Park" at Gilbert Carvalho Park in Hilo. Volunteers fire up a Portuguese brick oven and bake Portuguese white and sweet breads the old-fashioned way.

Evelyn Pacheco shows up faithfully on these occasions and bakes a big batch of tasty white bread. This recipe is based on the recipe she uses. However, I've expanded her simple list of ingredients with a great many explanations. Evelyn doesn't need any helpful advice, but novice bread cooks do.

*This is a big recipe. It's a lot of work to fire up a brick oven; you wouldn't do it for just a couple of loaves, but would bake for the week and share the oven with your neighbors, both of which the Portuguese housewives did.*

*If you have a small family, or don't want to knead by hand, there's a scaled-down recipe below.*

*In the old days lard was probably used in this recipe. However, if you are trying to limit the transfats in your diet and don't want to use shortening, you can substitute 1½ cups of olive oil, your favorite vegetable oil, or softened butter.*

(continued on page 24)

(continued from page 23)

Dissolve the yeast and 1 teaspoon sugar in the warm water in a large bread bowl. Let the yeast sit for a few minutes so that it can dissolve and start to grow.

Add the flour, sugar, salt, shortening and mix well. When the dough holds together well enough to knead, you can start kneading it in the bowl if you have a large, shallow, wooden bread bowl. Otherwise, you will have to turn the dough out onto a floured counter or bread board for kneading.

Knead by pushing the top part of the dough away from you with the heels of your hands. Grab the top of the dough and fold it back onto itself. Turn the dough a quarter turn and repeat. If the bread starts to stick, sprinkle a little more flour on the kneading surface.

Evelyn Pacheco tending a Portuguese oven at Gilbert Carvalho Park, courtesy of the Portuguese Chamber of Commerce.

When the dough is well kneaded, it should feel supple and springy. If you stretch it, you will see long strands of gluten, the protein in the bread flour. Let the dough rise in an oiled bowl, covered, until it has doubled in size. How long this takes will depend on the temperature and humidity; dough likes it hot and humid. Two hours is an average rising time. Punch it down and let it rise again.

When it has doubled in size, punch it down again and cut it into 8 equal-sized lumps if you are making loaf bread, or into smaller lumps if you are making dinner rolls or burger buns. Stretch and fold the dough lumps, then form them into loaves, rolls, or buns. Put the bread in oiled loaf pans, or put the rolls or buns on an oiled baking sheet. Cover the bread and let it rise until it doubles. This usually takes an hour or so. While it is rising, you can preheat your brick or kitchen oven. If you are baking loaves, you may want to slash the tops of the loaves before you put the bread in the oven. Just one lengthwise slash with a razor blade or a baker's lame, about ¼-inch deep, right down the middle, lets the bread rise even higher when it's put into the hot oven.

This bread is best baked in a brick oven. It's tricky to fire a brick oven and get just the right heat for baking; if this will be the first time you've done it, have an experienced brick oven baker at hand. Bakers usually use a peel, a sort of baker's shovel, to slide the loaves in and out of the oven. How long to bake it? That depends on the oven and how it's fired. You know that the bread is done when it has turned brown and sounds hollow when tapped.

If you don't have a brick oven, bake the bread in a regular gas or electric oven at 350°F for approximately 30 minutes. Again, it should be brown and sound hollow when tapped.

The bread will have a crisper crust if you put a pan full of water in your gas or electric oven as it is preheating; the water forms steam, which heats the crust. If you do this, watch out for the rush of steam when you open the oven door.

Take the loaves, rolls, or buns out of the oven when done. Remove them from the pans and cool them on wire racks. It's best to let the loaves cool to room temperature, for half an hour at a minimum, before you cut into them. They are still hot, and still cooking inside, when you take them from the oven. If you cut them early, the steam inside is released, the bread stops cooking, and the bread may become gummy and under-cooked. However . . . if your family just can't wait, give them one of the loaves and let the rest cool properly.

## PORTUGUESE WHITE BREAD ON A SMALL SCALE

**MAKES 2 LOAVES**

1 package (2¼ teaspoons) instant dry yeast
5 cups white bread flour
¼ cup sugar
1 teaspoon salt
⅓ cup melted shortening, olive oil, vegetable oil, or softened butter
1⅔ cups water

*If you don't want to make that much bread, here's a scaled-down recipe that you can knead in a sturdy stand mixer with a dough hook. You will want to make this in an electric or gas oven. It would be a waste of time and wood to fire up a brick oven to bake just two loaves!*

If you use instant dry yeast, you don't need to activate the yeast with water and sugar. Just mix everything together in a heavy-duty stand mixer with a dough hook, and knead for 9–10 minutes. The dough should cling to the dough hook and pull away from the sides of the bowl. It should be moist and stretchy. As flour can vary in its moisture content, it may take more or less flour to make the dough just right. Add a tablespoon or more of flour or water, in small installments, as needed. It makes a beautiful, pliable ball of dough!

Rise, form, slash, bake, and cool as in the larger recipe.

# HAMBURGER–ZUCCHINI JUN

**MAKES 6 SERVINGS**

1 pound hamburger
2 eggs, beaten
1 teaspoon salt
⅛ teaspoon black pepper
1 teaspoon sesame oil
2 tablespoons chopped
   green onion
   (approximately one stalk)
2 cups sliced zucchini,
   cut into ¼-inch circles
   (approximately 3–4 small
   zucchini)

**FOR FRYING**

2 eggs, beaten
½ cup flour
2 cups vegetable oil

## KOREAN CAMP

Korean laborers arrived in 1903. In 2003 a large and thriving Korean community celebrated one hundred years of progress for Hawai'i. Korean foods such as kim chee, kalbi, and taegu are now Big Island favorites.

*Korean cooks make many different foods into jun, or fried patties. Kay Okuda gave me this recipe for easy hamburger-zucchini jun.*

Mix the hamburger, 2 beaten eggs, salt, pepper, sesame oil, and chopped green onion. Mold 1 tablespoon of the hamburger mixture around each small zucchini slice. Roll the hamburger patties in the flour, then in the beaten eggs. Deep fry the tiny patties at 325°F for approximately 7–10 minutes, or until golden brown.

*Courtesy of Kay Okuda, Kay's Lunch Center*

# KAMOTE AND KAMATIS GULAY

MAKES 4 SERVINGS

2 pounds sweet potato
leaves (kamote)

2 cups thinly sliced tomato
(approximately 2 large
tomatoes)

2 cups thinly sliced onion
(approximately 1 small
onion)

1 teaspoon salt

2 tablespoons patis

1 teaspoon salad oil

## FILIPINO CAMP

The first 15 Filipino laborers came to Hawai'i in 1906. By 1920 there were 10,534 Filipinos in the Islands, forming 23% of the immigrant labor force. Many were bachelors who dreamed of making big money, returning to their homeland, buying a farm, and getting married. For all too many, however, those dreams went unfulfilled.

The traditional Filipino diet is a healthy one, featuring lots of fresh fish, fruits, and vegetables. Filipinos living in Hawai'i have maintained many of their healthy, thrifty ways. They have imported familiar plants like chayote and long beans, which are now found in many Island supermarkets. Typical Filipino seasonings include bagoong (salted and fermented fish or shrimp) and patis (the clear liquid drained off in the preparation of bagoong).

*Here's a healthy and tasty Filipino vegetable dish.*

Pick the tender kamote leaves from the stems and discard the stems. Blanch the leaves in boiling water. Do not overcook them. Drain the leaves in a colander. Combine all ingredients in a bowl and toss lightly to coat the leaves and tomatoes with the seasonings.

# MELTING POT

**ENOUGH** history lessons! Here are more local-kine recipes from various ethnic groups. Think of the chapter as a potluck. You know, the kind of potluck where you'll find macaroni salad and Filipino adobo, Japanese nishime and Portuguese sausage fried rice, Chinese noodles and pad Thai.

## MISO MARINATED SALMON

**MAKES 8 SERVINGS**

1 slab whole salmon fillet
  with skin, small bones
  removed with tweezers
½ cup white miso
¼ cup sugar
¼ cup mirin
¼ cup sake

*This main dish is a fine party dish because you must start it four days before the party. On the day of the party, you will only need to bake it. You can spend your remaining time preparing the other dishes on your menu.*

Whisk together the miso, sugar, mirin, and sake. Place the salmon and marinade in a 1-gallon re-sealable bag. Marinate for four days, turning once a day to be sure the salmon is marinated evenly.

Remove the salmon from the bag. Scrape off any excess miso. Bake the salmon in a 400°F oven for approximately 25 minutes, or until the center is cooked.

# NANTU

1 pound mochiko
2½ cups water

### SYRUP
2½ cups sugar
½ cup water
2 drops red food coloring

*Many East Asian cultures make delicious sweets from sweet rice or its flour. Here's an Okinawan treat made from the sweet rice flour most Hawai'i residents know by its Japanese name: mochiko.*

**To make the dough:** Put the water and mochiko into a large bowl and mix until you have a smooth dough. Wrap the dough in a damp dish towel. Put the bundle in a steamer and steam 45-60 minutes, or until mochi surface is shiny.

**To make the syrup:** Prepare the syrup while the mochi is steaming. Bring the sugar and water to a boil in a medium-size saucepan. Cook until the sugar is completely dissolved. Add 2 drops of red food coloring.

**To prepare the pan**: When you finish the syrup, and while the dough is still steaming, grease a 9 x 9-inch square pan. Flour it, not with regular wheat flour, but with katakuriko (potato starch) or a mixture of kinako (roasted soybean flour) and sugar. (Start with kinako and add sugar, bit by bit, until the mixture is to your taste.)

**To assemble the mochi:** When the dough has finished steaming, pour it into a mixing bowl, stir in the sugar syrup, and thoroughly mix the dough and syrup. Use a spoon rather than your mixer. Pour the mochi into the pan you have prepared. Cover with aluminum foil. Let the mochi set until it is completely cool. Use a plastic knife to cut the mochi into small pieces. Roll the pieces in katakuriko or kinako mixed with sugar. Wrap individually in squares of waxed paper. (The size and number of the wrappers needed will depend on the size of the cut pieces of nantu.)

# CHINESE STEAMED BUNS OR MANTOU

## MAKES 32 MANTOU

1 teaspoon active dry yeast

⅔ cup warm (100°F) water

1 teaspoon vegetable shortening (to grease a bowl)

3½ cups white all-purpose flour

1 tablespoon + 1 teaspoon sugar

3 teaspoons baking powder

2 tablespoons vegetable shortening (for the dough)

⅔ cup lukewarm milk

*These elegant buns are the perfect companion to fatty or spicy Chinese dishes. Breads and noodles made with wheat flour, such as the mantou, are typical of northern Chinese cooking, whereas southern Chinese recipes make more use of rice.*

Be sure to use all-purpose flour, or even a mixture of all-purpose and cake flour, rather than bread flour. Bread flour has a high gluten content. Low-gluten flour is better for mantou.

Dissolve the yeast in the warm water, and set it aside until foamy, or approximately 5 minutes.

Grease another bowl with 1 teaspoon shortening, set aside.

Sift the flour, sugar, and baking powder together. Using your fingers, work in 2 tablespoons shortening until the mixture resembles coarse meal. Add this flour mixture to the yeast mixture. Add the warm milk and stir the dough until it is stiff.

Turn the dough onto a floured board and knead until smooth, or about 15 minutes. Shape the dough into a ball and transfer it to the oiled bowl; cover the oiled bowl with plastic wrap. Set the dough aside in a warm place until it has doubled in size, or about 2 hours.

Grease the slats of bamboo steamer with oil so that the dough does not stick.

Divide the mantou dough into 32 balls and flatten them into 3-inch diameter disks. Brush the surface of the disks with canola oil, then fold the disks in half to form half-moon shaped buns. Let the shaped buns rest in the steamer basket for 15 minutes.

Steam the buns until they are light and puffy, or about 15 minutes. You can serve the buns with Chinese parsley sprigs, green onion strips, Chinese plum sauce, and mango chutney.

# CHICKEN NISHIME

½ cup boneless, skinless chicken breasts or thighs

2 pieces aburage (fried tofu), cut into 1-inch wedges

1 tablespoon canola oil

½ cup water (added during cooking)

1 strip nishime kombu, 36 inches long

1 cup wedge-cut gobo (burdock root)

1 cup wedge-cut carrots

1 cup chopped takenoko (bamboo shoots) (fresh if possible, but canned will do)

1 cup frozen satoimo

1 cup sliced lotus roots (¼-inch slices)

1 (6-ounce) block kamaboko (fish cake), cut into 1-inch wedges

¼ cup soy sauce

⅔ cup brown sugar

*Nishime, or Japanese stew, is a popular party and potluck dish. For many Big Island families it's a must-have to mark the New Year. Nishime is a tasty, healthy stew of meat or fish, seaweed, and assorted vegetables. There are many different versions of nishime. This is the one I like.*

*This recipe calls for satoimo, Colocasia esculenta var. esculenta, the underground tuber of a plant in the taro family. You might also find this in the produce section labeled "dasheen" or "Japanese taro." Since the oxalic acid crystals in fresh, raw satoimo can irritate your hands, take it easy and buy frozen satoimo. This is what everyone uses.*

You can give a Big Island twist to this recipe by adding fresh bamboo shoots picked from a local bamboo grove or purchased at the farmers' market. You can also add local kakuma, or fern shoots.

Look at the chopping directions before you measure and chop the ingredients. The visual appeal of this dish lies in the precisely cut ingredients. You will be cutting many of the ingredients into wedges. Make an angled cut to the left, then to the right, and repeat. Study the pictures carefully.

Most of the work is done when you have finished the chopping.

### To chop the ingredients:
- Cut the chicken into 1-inch cubes.
- Cut up the aburage.
- Soak the kombu in the water; when it has softened, tie the strip in knots every two inches. Cut between the knots.
- Scrape the skin from the gobo. Cut into wedges. Put the wedges into water to cover after cutting. Add 1 teaspoon of vinegar or lemon juice to the water and soak for at least 10 minutes. (Overnight would be OK too.) Drain before cooking.
- Peel the carrots, then cut them into wedges.
- Cut the takenoko in half, and then into ½-inch-thick slices.

- Scrape the skin off the lotus root and cut it into ¼-inch-thick slices. Immediately submerge the slices in water; add a teaspoon of vinegar or lemon juice. If you do not do this, the cut root will turn brown.

When all the ingredients are chopped, you'll have nine or more bowls lined up on the counter, ready to cook. The difficult part is pau; the rest is easy.

Pour the canola oil into a large pot and turn the heat to medium. When the oil is hot, add the chopped chicken and aburage; cook the mixture until the chicken turns white. Add the kombu, gobo, and the ½ cup water; simmer the mixture for 20 minutes. Add the carrots and bamboo shoots and simmer for another 5 minutes.

Add the satoimo but do not mix it into the nishime with a spoon. Give the entire pot a gentle shake to mix the vegetables. You must handle the satoimo gently or it will turn into mashed satoimo. Cook the stew until all the vegetables are tender. Shake the pot every 15 minutes. When the nishime is cooked, add the soy sauce and brown sugar, shake to mix, and serve.

# RED FISH WITH SOMEN

1 large red fish or 2 medium-
   sized menpachi, scaled
   and cleaned
½ cup soy sauce
1 cup water
2 tablespoons sugar
1 (9-ounce) package somen
2 tablespoons chopped
   green onions

*When Big Islanders of Japanese heritage celebrate an auspicious occasion, especially New Year's Day, they usually cook a red fish in nitsuke (shoyu and sugar) and serve it on a bed of somen. The red fish signifies good luck; the somen signifies long life.*

**To prepare the somen:** Cook the somen in boiling water until it is al dente. Drain in a colander and set aside.

**To prepare the sauce:** Put the soy sauce, water, and sugar into a medium-size saucepan and bring to a boil. Turn down the heat so that the sauce is just simmering.

**To cook the fish:** Put the cleaned fish in the sauce and cook 10 to 12 minutes.

**To serve:** Spread the somen on a serving platter. Carefully place the cooked fish on the somen. Pour the sauce over all; garnish the fish and somen with the green onions.

# HONTO RICE OR GANDULE RICE

**MAKES 20 SERVINGS**

1 cup vegetable oil

3 pounds pork shoulder, cut into ¼-inch cubes

2 tablespoons achiote or annatto seeds

2 cups chopped onions

2 cups chopped fresh cilantro

12 cloves garlic, crushed

2 tablespoons salt

2 teaspoons black pepper

2 (8 ounce) cans tomato sauce

1 (15 ounce) can pigeon peas, drained

1 (6 ounce) can pitted black olives, halved

8 cups uncooked short grain rice, rinsed

9 cups water

*Delicious with pasteles.*

Put 2 tablespoons of the oil in the bottom of a large stockpot and heat over medium-high heat. Add the pork cubes and brown them in the oil. Keep a close eye on them; don't let them burn, and turn them frequently to make sure that they are seared on all sides. When they are done, turn off the heat for the moment and make the achiote oil.

Place the remaining oil in a small saucepan over medium heat and add the achiote seeds. Keep heating the oil until it turns a dark orange-red. Don't overheat; the oil should not smoke. Remove the oil from the heat. Let it cool slightly, then strain the oil through a fine-mesh sieve. Discard the seeds, leaving the achiote oil.

Add the onion, cilantro, garlic, salt and pepper to the pork. Cook over medium heat until the vegetables are soft, then add the tomato sauce, peas, olives, and achiote oil. Stir well, turn the heat to low, and let the pork and vegetable mixture simmer for 10 minutes.

Add the 8 cups of uncooked rice and 9 cups of water to pork mixture and stir well. Turn the heat to high and bring the pork and rice to a boil. Stir again, reduce heat to low, and cover the pot. Let the rice cook on low for 10 minutes. Remove the pot lid, stir the mixture again, replace the lid, and cook for another 10 minutes. Then remove the pot from the heat and let it stand for 15 minutes. The heat retained by the pork and rice will finish cooking the rice.

# PORK GUISANTES OR PORK AND PEAS

MAKES 6 SERVINGS

1 pound lean pork
2 cloves garlic
1 tablespoon canola oil
1 teaspoon salt
3 dried bay leaves, crumbled
¼ teaspoon black pepper
1 cup sliced onion
   (approximately 1 medium-
   size onion)
½ cup water
1 (4 ounce) can tomato sauce
2 teaspoons chopped
   pimiento
2 cups frozen peas

*This is an easy, tasty Filipino dish. Serve it with rice and salad for a quick dinner.*

Heat the oil in a medium-size pot over medium-high heat. Sauté the pork and garlic until the pork is lightly browned. Add the salt, bay leaves, pepper, and onion, and lower the heat to medium. Stir the onion from time to time, and continue cooking until the onions are translucent. Add the ½ cup water and simmer the pork and onions until the water has evaporated. Taste; add more salt if necessary. Add the tomato sauce and chopped pimiento, then simmer for 3 minutes. Add the frozen peas, cook until the peas are thawed, mix well, and serve hot.

# PALUSAMI

MAKES 4 SERVINGS

1 bag taro or kalo leaves
1 (3-pound) can of New
    Zealand corned beef
6 medium-size limes
4 large onions, coarsely
    chopped
4 cans coconut milk

There is a growing community of Pacific Islanders on the Big Island. Tongans, Samoans, Fijians, Micronesians, and other Pacific Islanders feel at home in our already diverse community. Some come to study, as the University of Hawai'i at Hilo makes a special effort to attract Pacific Islanders. UH Hilo offers them scholarships, special tutoring, and out-of-state tuition waivers.

*Here's a recipe for Samoan palusami, or meat baked with onions and coconut milk. In Samoa this might be cooked in leaf-wrapped bundles in an imu, or earth oven, much as the Hawaiian laulau is cooked. In urban kitchens, Samoans make do with a regular oven.*

If you don't like corned beef, you can substitute 3 pounds of chicken, pork, or turkey.

If you are using frozen coconut milk, thaw the milk.

If you will be making this dish with chicken, pork, or turkey, prepare the meat. Remove all skin and bones and cut the meat into chunks no larger than one inch across. Sauté the meat in a large frying pan in several tablespoons of oil, then remove from the heat.

Juice 2 of the limes. You will need at least 2 tablespoons of lime juice.

Strip the stems from the taro leaves; discard the stems. Tear the leaves into 3 or 4 large pieces and arrange them to cover the bottom of a large roasting pan. Cover the leaves with a layer of corned beef (or other meat), then a layer of chopped onions. Drizzle the lime juice over the onions. Pour the coconut milk over the palusami.

Cover the roasting pan with foil and bake for 2 to 3 hours in a 350°F oven. Serve garnished with lime wedges.

# AKU WITH VINHA D'ALHOS

**MAKES 6 SERVINGS**

1 whole aku, 3-4 pounds,
  cleaned, filleted, skin on,
  head and tail removed

**MARINADE**

½ cup white vinegar

½ cup water or ¼ cup water
  + ¼ cup cooking wine

¼ cup olive oil

1 tablespoon Hawaiian salt

1 tablespoon minced garlic

1 Hawaiian chili pepper, or 2
  if you like "hot"

⅛ teaspoon black pepper

⅛ teaspoon allspice

¼ cup finely sliced onion
  (approximately ¼ of a
  medium-size onion)

*Vinha d'alhos is a Portuguese marinade for meat. It is made with wine, vinegar, oil, and various flavorings, and is usually used to marinate pork. Pork with vinha d'alhos is an Island favorite, and so familiar that if you say, "vinha d'alhos," most folks will assume that you're talking about marinated pork. However, the marinade can be used with other meats—or even, as in this Big Island dish, with fish. Portuguese on the Big Island marinate aku, or small tuna, in vinha d'alhos. This is an economical dish, as aku is much cheaper than the prized 'ahi, or large tuna.*

Place the aku in a large re-sealable plastic bag. Pour the marinade over the fish and close the bag. Let the bag stand in the refrigerator overnight. Turn the bag occasionally so that all parts of the fish are well marinated.

Put the fish in a 9 x 13-inch baking pan. Pour remaining marinade over fish. Cover with a lid or aluminum foil, and bake at 300°F for 1 hour. Baste the fish with the pan juices once or twice while baking.

Serve the fish with the thickened and reduced marinade as a sauce.

# PANIOLO TARO STEW

## MAKES 6 SERVINGS

¼ cup flour

½ teaspoon salt

¼ teaspoon black pepper

1 pound beef stew meat, cut into chunks no larger than 2 inches

2 tablespoons oil (approximately)

2 cups chopped onion (approximately 1 medium-size onion)

1 teaspoon crushed or grated ginger

1 clove garlic, minced

1 Hawaiian chili pepper, seeded and minced

5 cups water

2 cups chopped carrots, cut into 1-inch cubes (approximately 2 large carrots)

2 pounds cooked taro, peeled and cut into 1-inch cubes

1 cup chopped green onions

1 teaspoon Hawaiian salt

Poi to thicken, approximately ¼-½ cup (you can substitute cornstarch slurry if poi is unavailable)

Salt to taste

*Paniolos worked hard all day and relished a hearty dinner when they were pau hana. This paniolo taro stew hit the spot.*

*Be sure to boil or steam the taro before you peel and chop it. If you try to peel raw taro, your hands will itch.*

Combine the flour, salt, and pepper to make seasoned flour. Roll the chunks of stew meat in the flour mixture until they are covered with flour on all sides. If you have a pair of cooking chopsticks, roll the chunks with chopsticks. Otherwise, you can use your fingers.

Heat the oil in a large pot over medium-high heat. Brown the meat on all sides. Do not crowd the meat in the pot, as this lowers the temperature. The meat will simmer rather than brown. You may have to brown the meat in several batches.

When the meat is browned, add the onion, ginger, garlic, and water. Cover the pot, lower the heat, and simmer the stew for approximately 2 hours, or until meat is tender.

Add the chopped carrots and taro to the pot, cover, and simmer another 40 minutes or so. The carrots and taro should be soft but not mushy.

When you are ready to serve the stew, you can thicken it with poi. If you don't have poi on hand, a slurry of 1 tablespoon cornstarch mixed with 1 tablespoon cold water will thicken the dish nicely.

Add the Hawaiian salt and the chopped green onions just before serving.

# PANIOLO CHILI

## MAKES 6 SERVINGS

1 (12 ounce) Portuguese
    sausage, sliced into ¼-inch
    rounds

1 pound lean ground beef

2 cups chopped onion
    (approximately 1 large
    onion)

Oil for sautéing

2 (15 ounce) cans pork and
    beans, including sauce

1 (14.5 ounce) can stewed
    tomatoes, including juice

1 (11 ounce) can whole kernel
    corn, drained

1 (6 ounce) can olives,
    drained

1 (4 ounce) can mushrooms,
    either whole or stems and
    pieces, drained

1 (8 ounce can) tomato sauce

Salt to taste

Mexican cowboys (español, or paniolo in the Hawaiian language) were brought to the Big Island to teach Hawaiians how to herd and rope cattle. Native Hawaiians became superlative cowboys; one paniolo, Ikaika Purdy, won many mainland rodeo contests.

*The original paniolos also brought Mexican and Western U.S. campfire cuisine to Hawai'i. Here's an easy chili recipe made with canned ingredients, just the kind of food that would be carried in a chuckwagon.*

Coat the bottom of a large pot with cooking oil and heat over medium-high heat. Add the ground beef and onions; sauté. Break up any large chunks of meat. When the hamburger is cooked, add the sliced Portuguese sausage. Continue cooking until the sausage is slightly browned and the onions are soft.

Drain off any excess fat. Add the remaining ingredients. Lower the heat until the chili is just simmering. Simmer the stew for 25 minutes. Add salt to taste before serving.

This statue honors paniolo in front of Parker Ranch Shopping Center in Waimea.

# PIPIKAULA

**MAKES 2 POUNDS**

2 pounds flank steak

**MARINADE**

¾ cup soy sauce
2 tablespoons Hawaiian salt
1½ tablespoons sugar
1 clove garlic, minced
2 teaspoons crushed ginger
1 Hawaiian chili pepper,
    crushed

*Pipikaula is Hawaiian-style beef jerky. The Hawaiian name means, literally, beef rope.*

*This recipe uses flank steak to make a lean but tasty jerky. If you like to munch during the day, this makes a healthier snack than a candy bar.*

Cut the beef into strips: 1½-inch wide and ¼-inch thick.

Mix all the ingredients for the marinade. Put the beef and the marinade in a 1-gallon re-sealable bag and marinate the strips overnight. Turn the bag a few times, whenever you remember, so that all the strips are properly marinated.

The next day, remove the beef strips from the marinade. Drain them in a colander.

Pre-heat your oven to 175°F. Lay out the meat strips on racks laid out in a roasting pan. Thin wire cake-cooling racks are ideal. Bake the pipikaula for 7 hours. Remove from the oven and allow the jerky to cool to room temperature.

# PORTUGUESE BOILED DINNER

MAKES 6 SERVINGS

12 ounces Portuguese sausage (or more, if you like sausage)

1 cabbage

2 russet potatoes

3 carrots

2 pipinola squash (pipinola is also called chayote)

2 large garlic cloves

1-2 chili peppers

2 tablespoons Hawaiian salt

*This is a simple and delicious Portuguese one-pot dish. You could easily prepare it in a slow cooker. Imagine coming home from a long day at work to find this waiting for you!*

*You can also vary the dish by adding two or more cups of cooked beans to the pot. Kidney beans work well. You can use canned beans, but if you do, drain and rinse them to remove some of the "canned" taste.*

*As this stew doesn't require exact quantities of anything, I've called for quantities such as 1 cabbage, or 3 carrots. As vegetables can vary greatly in size, you'll have to use your own judgment as to whether you'll use all of a large head of cabbage, say, or add more cabbage if the cabbage is small. If you like this dish and make it often, you'll soon tune the recipe to your taste.*

Cut the potatoes, carrots, and squash into large chunks; cut the cabbage into quarters. Layer all the ingredients in a large pot or crock-pot and add enough water to cover the vegetables. Cook 2 hours on medium in a slow cooker or 3 hours on low.

# CHICKEN LONG RICE

**MAKES 20 SERVINGS**

5 pounds chicken thighs, skin and visible fat removed

1 large round onion, chopped into ½ inch cubes

½ cup sliced ginger (quarter-size slices)

3 bay leaves

Salt to taste

7 ounces long rice (rice thread)

1 bunch green onions, sliced, or about ½ cup

*There are many versions of this local favorite. This version is simple and easy, but full of flavor.*

Place the chicken thighs in a large stockpot and add water to cover. Bring to a boil over medium-high heat. Add the onion, ginger, and bay leaves. Simmer the chicken until it is tender, or about one hour. Remove the pot of chicken from the heat and let it cool. Put a large colander in a large bowl and pour the contents of the pot into the colander. You should be left with a colander full of chicken and a bowl of chicken broth.

Remove the bay leaves and ginger residue, salt the broth to taste, put it back into the pot, and return the pot to the stove. Bring the broth back to a simmer. Add the long rice to the broth and continue to simmer.

While the rice threads are plumping and softening, prepare the chicken. Remove the bones and cut the meat into bite-sized pieces. When the long rice has softened, add the chicken pieces to the pot. Adjust the seasoning. Top with the sliced green onions and serve.

The Farmers Market at Volcano's Cooper's Center.

# SLOW COOKER LAULAU

**MAKES 10 SERVINGS**

4 pounds pork butt

2 pieces salted butterfish, about 6 ounces

2 large bunches lūʻau leaves, about 2 pounds

1 cup chicken broth

*The slow cooker laulau isn't as pretty as the traditional imu laulau, but it's a lot easier to cook.*

Remove the stems from the lūʻau leaves. Place the leaves in your microwave and heat them on high for 5 minutes, or until the leaves have wilted.

Put half of the leaves in the bottom of your slow cooker. Layer the pork butt and then the butterfish over the leaves. Top everything with the remaining leaves. Pour the chicken broth over the contents of the pot. Cover, turn the cooker to high, and keep it on high until the contents boil. Turn down the heat and simmer the laulau for 6 to 8 hours.

# CHAPTER 3

# THE BIG ISLAND EATS OUT

**YOU'LL** find the expensive, fancy restaurants in another chapter, "Celebrations." This chapter is dedicated to restaurants that have good food but not a lot of chic. Tourists may ignore these, but locals know them as good grinds.

A few Big Island favorites are family restaurants that have been run by the same family for two or three generations. Some of them have only been open for a few years, many have pleasant but unpretentious décor, and some are holes in the wall. All of them have great food.

Always remember what they say about a good Chinese restaurant: if there are a lot of Chinese customers, old and young, then the restaurant must be good. The same holds true for a good local restaurant on the Big Island. Look to see if the customers are locals. That is the sign!

# STEAMED MULLET, CHINESE STYLE

**MAKES 1 SERVING**

(One order of steamed mullet is either one 1-pounder or 2 smaller mullet)

1 pound mullet, cleaned, scales removed

2 tablespoons diagonally sliced green onions (approximately 2 fat stalks)

2 teaspoons peeled, sliced, and slivered fresh ginger (approximately 2 quarter-sized slices)

¼ cup chopped Chinese parsley (cilantro)

¼ cup soy sauce

¼ cup peanut oil

1 tablespoon sesame oil

Dash of ground white pepper

Ti leaves for steaming

## SEASIDE RESTAURANT

Seiichi and Matsumo Nakagawa opened the Seaside Restaurant in 1921, calling it the Seaside Club. The 1946 tsunami destroyed it, but it was quickly rebuilt and has been operating ever since. The restaurant is famed for its fresh fish. Chef Colin Nakagawa and his dad, Susumu, own a fish farm where they raise mullet, āholehole, catfish, golden tilapia, rainbow trout, carp, and pāpio for the restaurant. Fresh-caught mahimahi or ʻōpakapaka are often on the menu too. Here's one popular Seaside dish.

*To steam the fish:* Wrap the cleaned mullet in ti leaves and tie the leaf bundle firmly with twine; the fish should be completely enclosed. Steam the fish for 25 minutes or until done. Remove the fish from the leaf wrapping, remove the excess water from the leaves, and arrange some or all of the leaf on the serving plate. Put the fish on top of the leaves.

*To garnish the fish:* Sprinkle the fish with a dash of white pepper, then scatter the green onions and ginger over the top. Heat the peanut and sesame oil together until the oil starts to smoke. Pour the hot oil over the fish. If the oil is hot enough, the fish will sizzle. Careful how you pour; the oil could burn. Drizzle with soy sauce and garnish with the chopped cilantro.

*Courtesy of Seaside Restaurant*

# ERILEI'S FRIED RICE

**MAKES 6 TO 8 SERVINGS**

2-3 cups cold cooked rice

**MEAT MIX**
¼ cup diced bacon
¼ cup diced Portuguese
    sausage
¼ cup diced SPAM®
Dash of oil

**MISO MIX**
¼ cup miso
1 tablespoon grated onion
1 tablespoon grated garlic
1 tablespoon grated ginger

**SAUCE**
¼ cup soy sauce
¼ cup sugar
¼ cup water
1 teaspoon crushed red
    pepper

**GARNISH**
1 cup omelet shreds (see
    recipe page 5)
2 tablespoons julienned
    green onions
2 tablespoons julienned
    kamaboko

## CRONIES

Cronies opened in 1998 as a sports bar and grill. It's a popular place for lunch or dinner. Here's their recipe for fried rice, which is unusual in that it uses miso.

*EriLei's fried rice comes together quickly, so have all ingredients ready.*

Mix all the meat mix ingredients and set aside.

Mix all the miso mix ingredients and set aside.

Mix all the sauce ingredients and set aside.

Sliver all the garnishes, mix, and set aside.

Heat the dash of oil in a large frying pan; sauté the meat mix until the bacon is completely cooked. Add miso mixture; mix and cook for a minute or so. Add the rice and a little bit of the sauce. Keep cooking and stirring. If you'd like more color and taste, add more sauce.

**To serve**: Fill a bowl with the fried rice. Garnish with the slivered egg, green onion, and kamaboko. Enjoy!

*Courtesy of Cronies*

# OKINAWAN SHOYU PORK OR RAFUTE

**MAKES 10 TO 12 SERVINGS**

1 (approximately 7 pounds)pork butt

7 (1 inch long) chunks of ginger, peeled

7 cloves garlic, smashed

1 cup awamori (Okinawan sake) or regular dry sake

2 cups sugar

2 cups soy sauce (shoyu)

Vegetable oil, enough to coat the pan

Hawaiian chili pepper to taste

**Serving suggestions:**
On a bed of blanched won bok or any other cabbage topped off with chopped green onions. Drizzle sauce from pot over the pork and serve.

## NORI'S SAIMIN

Beth Ann Nishijima visited Hilo in 1983 to attend her mother's wedding. Noticing that there was no late-night saimin restaurant in Hilo, she saw a commercial opportunity. She soon moved to Hilo and opened Nori's Saimin.

When Beth Ann had just opened, she was asked to cook an Okinawan dinner. She cooked the rafute (pronounced raf'te) included here. It was such a success that she has served it at Nori's Saimin ever since.

*This recipe uses chunks of ginger rather than the familiar sliced or grated ginger. If you prefer, you can take the ginger out before you serve the rafute.*

Trim the excess fat from the pork butt and discard. Cut the pork into chunks, cutting against the grain. The chunks should measure approximately 3 x 7 inches.

Heat the vegetable oil in a Dutch oven or a deep pot with a cover. Add the garlic and three chunks of ginger. Add the pork and brown it on all sides. Do not crowd the pork in the pot; if you do, it will steam rather than brown. You will probably have to brown the pork in several batches. When all the pork has been browned, return it to the pot. Add the sugar, soy sauce, and the rest of the ginger, and bring to a boil for about 10-15 minutes. Before it begins to caramelize or thicken, add the sake, let it cook another 10 minutes.

Finally, add the chili pepper, turn the heat to simmer, place lid on the pot, let simmer for 30 minutes or until pork is tender. Before cutting the pork, let it sit for 15 minutes. The pork should be very tender. If you want the sauce to be a little thicker, just add a bit more sugar, and heat again on high.

*Courtesy of Nori's Saimin*

# CHICKEN PAPAYA

**MAKES 6 SERVINGS**

2 pounds boneless, skinless chicken thighs, cut into 2-inch pieces

1 tablespoon canola oil

1 teaspoon salt

1 tablespoon patis (Filipino fish sauce)

1 chunk ginger, 2 inches long, peeled

1 clove garlic, minced

2 cans (14.5 ounce) chicken broth

2 medium-size green papaya, seeded and cut into 2-inch cubes

## K'S DRIVE-IN

Giichi and Shika Kadota, together with their son Thomas and his wife, Kay, ran a small mom-and-pop store turned restaurant in Hilo until the 1960 tsunami

destroyed their building and their business. With typical Big Island determination they re-opened in 1964 as K's Drive-In. Forty-four years later, this restaurant is still a Hilo favorite. It is now run by Thomas Kadota's son, Dale. Three hard-working generations have made K's a Big Island landmark.

The two most popular plate lunches at K's are the pork cutlet and the chicken papaya. Dale Kadota kindly agreed to share his family's chicken papaya recipe.

*If you're wondering about the piece of ginger, yes, it's large, and yes, it's left whole. It's served with the chicken, and locals know to eat around it. If you're worried that a guest will mistakenly bite into it, you can remove it before serving.*

Heat the oil in a large saucepan or sauté pan over medium-high heat. Brown the chicken pieces on all sides. Add the salt, patis, and ginger to the chicken, and cook for 5 minutes, stirring occasionally. Add the chicken broth, cover, and cook the chicken for another 30 minutes. Add the papaya cubes and cook for another 15 minutes, or until the papaya is tender.

Good served over rice.

*Courtesy of K's Drive-In*

# LOCO MOCO

### CAFÉ 100

The absolute mos' famous Big Island dish is loco moco. Loco moco was invented in Hilo in 1949. Teens from the Lincoln Wreckers Athletic Club hung out at a restaurant called the Lincoln Grill, just across from Lincoln Park. Loco moco was sold for twenty-five cents to football players who requested a tasty and filling dish but couldn't afford to pay a lot for it.

Café 100 registered the loco moco name. Nowadays, when we think of loco moco, we might think of Hilo's Café 100, which specializes in the dish. There are usually twenty varieties of loco moco on sale, dishes like: bacon loco; chili loco; mahimahi loco; smoked sausage loco; stew loco; teriyaki loco; oyako loco; hot dog loco; and SPAM® loco. If the special of the day is chicken chop suey, the special loco of the day may be chicken chop suey loco.

Café 100 was opened in 1946 by Richard Miyashiro, who named the restaurant to honor his fellow soldiers from the 100th Battalion. The tsunami of 1946 destroyed the restaurant only three months after it was opened. Richard rebuilt his dream restaurant in 1960. Twenty-seven days later it was destroyed in the 1960 tsunami. Café 100 re-opened in 1962 at its present location, 969 Kilauea Avenue.

*Loco moco is rice, hamburger, egg, and gravy. It's fairly easy to get the rice and egg right, although the hamburger and gravy are harder.*

(continued on page 56)

(continued from page 55)

## GRAVY STOCK
2 pounds beef bones
1 carrot, diced
1 onion, diced
2 stalks celery, diced

## GOOD GRAVY
¼ cup flour
¼ cup melted butter
1½ cups gravy stock, from
    stock pot
Salt and pepper to taste

## HAMBURGER PATTIES FOR
## LOCO MOCO
2 pounds lean ground beef
1½ teaspoons salt
¼ teaspoon black pepper
1 egg, beaten
½ cup chopped onion
¼ cup milk
½ cup bread crumbs

## LOCO MOCO
## MAKES 1 SERVING
1 cup hot cooked rice
1 large fried hamburger
    patty
1 egg, cooked sunny side up
¼ cup brown gravy

**Prepare gravy stock:** Good gravy starts with a good stock. Put the diced carrots, onion, and celery in a baking pan. Place the beef bones on top and bake the pan in a 400°F oven for 45 minutes, until the bones are browned. Put the vegetables and bones in a large stock pot, add water to cover, and boil for 1 hour.

**Prepare gravy:** Whisk the flour into the melted butter over medium heat. Cook until flour and butter form a smooth paste; it should be hot enough to bubble a little. Slowly add the beef stock, stirring constantly so that no lumps form. Simmer for 10 minutes, or until the gravy begins to thicken. Season with salt and pepper to taste.

**Prepare hamburger patties:** Combine all ingredients and form into patties.

**To assemble:** Put the rice in a large bowl. Put a hamburger patty on top, add the cooked egg, and then pour the gravy over the egg.

Sound simple? As you see, it's not.

*Courtesy of Café 100*

# FRESH YOGURT SAUCE

1 gallon + 1 quart whole milk
1 tablespoon plain yogurt
¼ cup grated cucumber
   (measure after you have
   squeezed out the water)
1 tablespoon minced garlic
2 pinches salt
4 tablespoons dill weed

*You could also use
store-bought yogurt
(approximately ½ gallon)
for this sauce. However, it
won't have quite the same
fresh tang as yogurt you
make yourself.*

## PUKA PUKA KITCHEN

Puka Puka Kitchen can be found on Hilo's Kamehameha Avenue. It's a great place for bento-to-go, but you can also stop off for a nice lunch or early dinner.

Chef Randy Ishimine serves fried falafel with yogurt sauce as an appetizer. He is often asked for the yogurt sauce recipe; here it is. It's nice as a salad dressing or sandwich spread as well as a garnish for falafel.

*The yogurt bacilli need to be kept at a temperature of 110 to 115°F for six to eight hours to digest the milk. If your yogurt doesn't set, make sure that your starter is active (many commercial yogurts advertise this on the carton) and that you are keeping the temperature within the indicated limits. Too hot, and you kill the bacilli; too cold, and they won't grow. If your yogurt fails, you can always boil the milk again and repeat the process.*

**To make your own yogurt:** Pour the milk into a large pot; cook over medium heat until small bubbles just start to form along the edge of the milk. Cool the milk to approximately 115 to 118°F (use a cooking thermometer to check). Add 1 tablespoon plain yogurt. Divide the inoculated milk evenly between two ½-gallon containers. Wrap each container with a bath towel and put them in the refrigerator overnight.

The next day, open the yogurt containers and pour the thickened mixture through a fine sieve. The liquid that pours off, the whey, can be used in soup or just discarded. What is left in the sieve is your yogurt. Put the sieved yogurt into a large bowl and add the grated cucumber, garlic, salt, and dill weed. Mix and serve with falafel, or over a fresh salad.

*Courtesy of Puka Puka Kitchen*

# TOMATO BEEF

## MAKES 4–5 SERVINGS

1¼ pounds beef
2 stalks celery
1 stalk green onion
1 round onion
4 medium tomatoes, each
   cut into 6 wedges
Oil for cooking

### MARINADE

4 teaspoons sherry
2 tablespoons soy sauce
1 tablespoon cornstarch
2 tablespoons oil
2 tablespoons sugar

### SAUCE

2 tablespoons soy sauce
¾ cup ketchup
½ cup sugar
3 tablespoons Worcestershire
   sauce
½ cup water

## DON'S GRILL

In 1988 Don Hoota built his new restaurant on Hinano Street. It was a strikingly modern building at the time. Twenty years later the building is still there and the restaurant is still a local favorite.

*This recipe for Tomato Beef makes enough to feed a large 'ohana.*

*By the way, don't be surprised if you hear a Hilo native call this dish "Beef Tomato." Long-time Hilo folk have a trick of reversing words. For instance, they eat "ice shave" rather than shaved ice. Dunno why; perhaps a linguist could explain it.*

Cut the beef into thin strips across the grain. Mix all marinade ingredients. Marinate the beef for at least half an hour. Longer is better. If the beef is going to marinate longer than an hour, put the beef in the refrigerator in a covered container.

Cut the celery into ¼-inch slices. Cut the green onion into ½-inch slices, on the bias. Roughly chop the round onion into ½-inch chunks.

Pour just enough oil into a large sauté pan or skillet to cover the bottom of the pan. Put the pan over medium-high heat. Quickly stir-fry the marinated beef, then remove it from the pan.

Put the chopped celery, green onions, and round onions into the still-hot pan. Add the sauce. Bring them to a boil. Put the meat back in the pot. Cook until the celery and round onions are tender.

***To serve:*** Add the chopped tomatoes just before serving. Serve over rice or noodles.

(Vegetable quantities are approximate, as vegetables vary in size. Adjust quantities to taste.)

*Courtesy of Don's Grill*

# TARO CORNED BEEF HASH

**MAKES 8 SERVINGS**

2½ pounds taro
1 (12 ounce) can corned beef
Salt and pepper to taste

## KUHIO GRILLE AND ENCORE RESTAURANT

Whenever a Big Islander has a yearning for a one-pound laulau, they either go to Kuhio Grille at the Prince Plaza or to Restaurant Encore at Puainako Town Center in Hilo. Both restaurants are run by the Araki family and feature the same great laulaus.

Tom Araki and his wife, Sueno, ran the Tom Araki Hotel in Waipio Valley; they also raised taro. While they sold much of their taro, they always saved some for laulaus. Sueno's laulau recipe is still a family secret.

Their son Sam Araki opened one, then two, restaurants in Hilo, serving the famous Araki laulaus. Although Sam no longer works the old Araki taro fields, he and wife, Nelline, with help from their daughters, are able to get a steady supply of taro leaves for their laulaus from other local farmers.

I can't give you the laulau recipe, but the Arakis were willing to share some other 'ono recipes from their restaurants.

Steam the taro for 3 hours or until the corms are thoroughly cooked, even in the middle. Larger taro corms may take longer; smaller ones may be done more quickly. Peel the skin from the taro corms. Use a grater with large holes to grate the taro flesh. Put the grated taro into a large bowl.

Add the whole can of corned beef to the taro. Salt and pepper to taste. Mix well.

To cook, form the taro-beef mixture into 3-inch-diameter balls. Flatten the balls. Pan fry them in a little oil, just enough to coat the pan. Cook on both sides and serve hot.

*Courtesy of Kuhio Grille and Encore Restaurant*

# KĀLUA PORK OMELET

MAKES 1 SERVING

3 large eggs
½ cup kālua pork (see recipe on page 4)
¼ cup fresh tomatoes, seeded and diced
¼ cup diced round onion
1 ounce Swiss cheese, grated or cut into thin slices

## ENCORE RESTAURANT

Encore Restaurant in the Puainako Shopping Center made the first kālua pork omelet when a customer asked for one. The dish was a hit and has been on the menu ever since.

Coat the bottom of a frying pan with a little oil. Heat the oil over medium heat.

Beat 3 eggs in a bowl.

When the pan is hot enough, pour the beaten eggs into the pan.

Spread the pork, tomatoes, onion, and cheese over half of the omelet. Cover the pan.

When the eggs have set firmly, fold the omelet in half.

Serve hot with rice.

*Courtesy of Encore Restaurant*

# PORK TOFU

**MAKES 4 SERVINGS**

1 tablespoon canola oil

½ pound lean pork, cut into thin strips

2 garlic cloves, finely minced

1 teaspoon ground bean sauce

1½ cups chicken broth

2 teaspoons oyster sauce

2 teaspoons soy sauce

¼ teaspoon salt

½ teaspoon raw sugar

1 (12–14 ounce) block tofu, cut into 1-inch cubes

2 tablespoons cornstarch

2 stalks green onion, chopped into ¼-inch lengths

## SUM LEUNG CHINESE KITCHEN

In 1969 Sum and Shun Nuen Leung immigrated from Hong Kong to Honolulu, where Sum worked in several Chinatown restaurants. In 1971 they moved to Hilo, and four years later they opened Leung's Chop Suey House. In 1978 they moved the restaurant to the KTA Shopping Center and started using the name Sum Leung Chinese Kitchen.

Mr. Leung died suddenly in 1981, but Mrs. Leung and her four young children were able to keep the restaurant going. Today, the Leung family still runs the restaurant, which is now a busy Hilo favorite.

Ellen Leung shared their popular pork tofu recipe.

*You may substitute shrimp or beef for the pork, or even leave out the pork for a meatless dish.*

Heat the oil in a large frying pan. When the oil is hot, add the pork and sauté until brown. Lower the heat to medium and add the ground bean sauce and the garlic. Stir; do not let garlic brown.

Add the chicken stock and stir. Add the soy sauce, oyster sauce, salt, and raw sugar; cook and stir. Add the cubed tofu. Raise the heat slightly and let the dish boil. Lower the heat again.

Mix the 2 tablespoons of cornstarch with ½ tablespoon cold water. Slowly pour the cornstarch slurry into the pan, mixing it gently with the pork tofu. If you mix too vigorously, you'll break the tofu into bits.

Put the pork tofu in a serving dish and garnish with chopped green onions. Good over rice or noodles.

*Courtesy of Sum Leung Chinese Kitchen*

# PORK ADOBO

MAKES 12-14 SERVINGS

1 (approximately 7 pounds)
    pork butt (you can
    substitute 5 pounds of
    chicken thighs)

1 tablespoon salt

1 teaspoon black pepper
    (table grind)

1 tablespoon whole black
    peppercorns

3 whole bay leaves

1 teaspoon onion salt

3 tablespoons apple cider
    vinegar

1 tablespoon soy sauce

1 tablespoon chopped garlic

1 medium-size potato

2 tablespoons vegetable oil

Water

## HIRO'S PLACE

Hiroshi Tanaka opened Hiro's Place in 1990. Hiroshi's wife, Sachiko, and their daughter, Naomi, are now running the restaurant, which is currently located in Hilo's

KTA Shopping Center. Many KTA Puainako employees eat breakfast, lunch, and dinner there on the way to and from the employee parking lot.

Hiro's Place specializes in Filipino, Japanese, and local favorites. Here is their recipe for pork adobo.

Cut the pork into 1-inch cubes.

Peel the potato and cut it into 1-inch cubes.

Heat the oil in the bottom of a large pot over medium heat. When the oil is hot, add the garlic and cook for 1 minute. Add the pork cubes and brown on all sides. You may need to do this in several batches. Put all the pork back in the pot and add water to cover. Add the bay leaves, black pepper (ground and whole), salt, onion salt, apple cider vinegar, and the soy sauce. Boil the pork for 1 hour.

Add the cubed potato and boil for another 15 minutes, or until meat and potatoes are tender and soft.

*Courtesy of Hiro's Place*

# OGO NAMASU

**MAKES 4 TO 6 SERVINGS**

¼ cup sugar
3 tablespoons vinegar
1 teaspoon salt
1 medium onion, sliced
1 medium tomato, cubed
1 pound ogo
Sesame oil to taste
Soy sauce to taste

### MANAGO HOTEL

Manago Hotel, in the town of Captain Cook on the Kona Coast, opened in 1919, originally just as a restaurant. When traveling salesmen came to eat they asked Mrs. Manago where they could sleep. She would lay out futons, or Japanese mattresses, on the second floor and charge them for the night's stay. This proved to be profitable, so they opened a hotel.

They moved to their present location in 1929. Eighty years later the hotel and the restaurant are still open, and still run by the Manago family.

The Manago Restaurant is famous for its pork chops. The recipe for the pork chops is incredibly simple: season the chops with salt and pepper, coat with breadcrumbs, and cook in an iron skillet. Simple or not, it takes a lot of practice to make a perfect Manago Hotel pork chop!

Their ogo namasu (seaweed salad) is a long-time customer favorite. Regulars call Dwight Manago and his staff to find out when the namasu will be served. Dwight buys the ogo from Hawaiian Sea Farms at Keahole, Kona.

Bring a large pot of water to a boil. Drop the ogo in the pot. As soon as the ogo turns green, remove it from the water, drain it, and rinse it in cold water.

Put the ogo in a large bowl. Add sesame oil and soy sauce to taste.

Make the sauce by mixing the sugar, vinegar, and salt. Stir the sauce until the sugar and salt are completely dissolved. Add the sauce to the ogo, then the sliced onions and cubed tomato. Mix well and serve.

*Courtesy of Manago Hotel*

# TEMPURA BATTER FOR SHRIMP AND FISH

### MAKES 1 CUP BATTER

1 cup cake flour
¼ cup cornstarch
2 teaspoons baking powder
¼ teaspoon baking soda
Ice water or club soda to wet batter
Canola oil for deep frying

### TESHIMA STORE

Teshima Store opened in 1929 in Honalo, Kona. It was a grocery store at first, and in 1940 it became a restaurant.

Grandma Teshima, one of the original owners, is still alive. She will be 101 in June 2008. I very much enjoyed sitting with her and hearing her stories. In the old days, she told me, there were no electric refrigerators, so she ordered ice from Hilo in order to make ice cream to sell. She also made her own saimin noodles and dashi. When she was 50 she opened a nightclub where King Kamehameha Hotel now stands. She was the first restaurant owner on the Big Island to bring professional cooks over from Japan. She wanted to train her staff in gourmet Japanese cooking.

Teshima Store is still owned by the Teshima family. Fourth generation Teshimas work in the restaurant. Tempura is one of their most popular dishes. They added this caution when I asked about their recipe: just having the right batter isn't enough to make good tempura; the temperature of the frying oil is critical. If it is not hot enough, the tempura will be soggy. If it is too hot, the batter will brown but the interior will not be cooked. Watch that frying thermometer!

Mix dry ingredients, then add iced water or club soda until the batter is approximately the consistency of heavy cream. The batter should be lighter than pancake batter. It is OK if the batter is a bit lumpy.

***To prepare simple fried fish or shrimp:*** Season the fish with salt and pepper before dipping it into batter. Shrimp does not need to be seasoned. Be sure your oil is at 375°F before frying. Fry until golden brown and drain on paper towels.

*Courtesy of Teshima Store*

# TARO PUFFS

**MAKES 3 DOZEN PUFFS**

1 pound taro or taro root,
    cooked and mashed

1 cup sugar

¼ cup flour

½ cup mochiko (glutinous
    rice flour)

Cooking oil as needed

## KONA HOTEL

Zentaro and Hatsuyo Inaba opened the Kona Hotel in Holualoa in 1926. Today Mrs. Yayoko Inaba runs the hotel, which is now painted a dazzling hot pink. The hotel is known for its amazing outhouse, built on a ridge and commanding a spectacular view of the Kona Coast.

The Kona Hotel was known for its taro puffs. The hotel no longer serves them, but Mrs. Inaba still has the family recipe and was willing to share it with us.

*As you probably know by now, raw taro root will irritate your hands. Many Big Islanders steam the whole taro first and only peel and slice it after cooking.*

Mix all ingredients in a large bowl. Heat cooking oil to 375°F in a heavy skillet (oil should be ½-inch deep, at least) or a deep fryer. Slip spoonfuls of the taro batter into the oil and deep fry until golden brown. Drain the puffs on paper towels. Serve hot.

*Courtesy of Kona Hotel*

# CHICKEN SATAY POT-STICKERS

**MAKES APPROXIMATELY
20 POT-STICKERS**

1 package (12 ounces) ready-
made wonton wrappers
(get extra; it's better to run
out of filling than it is to
run out of wrappers)

### FILLING

1 pound ground chicken

2 tablespoons minced garlic

2 tablespoons minced fresh
ginger

2 tablespoons minced
shallots

1 cup chunky peanut butter

¼ cup brown sugar

2 tablespoons hot chili paste

2 tablespoons chopped fresh
basil

2 tablespoons chopped fresh
cilantro

### CHILI MINT SAUCE

1 (10 ounce) bottle of Thai
sweet chili sauce

¼ cup rice vinegar

½ cup sugar

¼ cup chopped cilantro

¼ cup chopped fresh mint

1 teaspoon sesame oil

## BAMBOO RESTAURANT

Bamboo Restaurant and Gallery opened in 1993. It's located in Hāwī town, North Kohala, in the old Harada Hotel. This pūpū is a customer favorite.

*To prepare the filling:* Coat the bottom of a large sauté pan or skillet with cooking oil and put the pan over medium-high heat. When the oil is hot, sauté the garlic and ginger, then add the chicken. Stir and cook until the chicken is thoroughly cooked. Remove the pan from the heat. Drain off any excess fat.

Scrape the chicken into a large bowl and add the peanut butter, sugar, chili paste, and herbs. Mix well, then put in the refrigerator to chill.

*To prepare the chili mint sauce:* Purée all ingredients in a food processor for approximately 1 minute. Serve at room temperature. Any leftover sauce should be stored in the refrigerator.

*To assemble the pot-stickers:* Put 1½ teaspoons (a heaping teaspoon) of the chicken filling in the center of a wonton wrapper. Put a dab of water on the edges of the wrapper and close the wrapper. You can fold the wrapper into a tri-angle or you can try bringing all the corners together and pinching them shut. Experiment to find the shape that is best for you. Fold the pot-stickers until you run out of filling.

Put the completed pot-stickers in a steamer and steam for 8-10 minutes, or until the wrappers are translucent.

You can serve them simply steamed, with chili mint dipping sauce. You may also want to fry the pot-stickers in hot oil before serving.

*Courtesy of Bamboo Restaurant*

# BACON NOODLES

MAKES 4 SERVINGS

3-4 strips crisp bacon

1 (6 ounce) package chuka soba noodles

2 tablespoons finely julienned fresh ginger

½ cup bias-cut green onions (approximately 1 bunch)

2 teaspoons minced garlic

2 tablespoons sesame oil

1 cup chicken stock

1 cup julienned carrot (approximately 1 carrot)

1 cup bias-cut celery (approximately 2 stalks)

1 cup finely chopped onion

1 cup julienned zucchini (approximately 1 zucchini)

2 tablespoons oyster sauce

4 tablespoons soy sauce

## THE 19TH HOLE AT MAUNA KEA RESORT

The 19th Hole Restaurant at the Mauna Kea Resort is a relaxed hangout for tired golfers. Chef Piet Wigmans, Executive Chef of Mauna Kea Resort, shared the recipe for this down-home noodle dish with me.

Soak the noodles in the chicken stock until they soften.

Heat the sesame oil in a large sauté pan or skillet. Add the diced bacon and cook until crisp.

Add the carrot, celery, onion, and zucchini and stir-fry. Keep the heat up; the vegetables should cook quickly and stay crisp.

Add the noodles and stock, the oyster sauce, and the soy sauce. Continue cooking until most of the liquids have evaporated. Stir and toss the noodles as they cook. Serve piping hot.

*Courtesy of Chef Piet Wigmans, The 19th Hole at Mauna Kea Resort*

# CAPTAIN'S SEAFOOD PASTA

**MAKES 6 SERVINGS**

12 mussels

12 scallops (medium to large)

12 clams

12 shrimp (jumbo; 21/25)

12 ounces mahimahi or other
white fish

1 cup sliced mushrooms
(approximately one
8 ounce supermarket
container)

1 teaspoon minced fresh
garlic

2 tablespoons chopped fresh
basil

1 teaspoon chopped fresh
shallots

¼ cup dry white wine

1 tablespoon unsalted butter

2 tablespoons olive oil

Salt and pepper to taste

12 ounces fettuccine
noodles

1 tablespoon sliced green
onions for garnish
(optional)

Uncle Billy's Restaurant has been serving customers on Hilo's Banyan Drive since 1968. It is the only restaurant in Hilo to have live entertainment nightly, so when Big Islanders have visitors, they will often bring the visitors to Uncle Billy's for a pleasant meal and a hula show. There's an Uncle Billy's Restaurant in Kona too.

Uncle Billy, courtesy of Aaron Whiting of Uncle Billy's.

The seafood pasta is a customer favorite. Here's a version of the dish from Aaron Whiting, Uncle Billy's grandson.

Bring a large pot of water to a boil and add the noodles. Cook until al dente. Drain the noodles, then set them aside until it is time to serve the dish.

Wipe the mushrooms with a damp cloth, to clean them, then remove the stems and chop finely. Cut the caps into thin slices.

Cut the fish into 12 (1 ounce) pieces; the pieces should be approximately the same size as the other bits of seafood, so that they all cook at the same rate.

Coat the bottom of a large sauté pan with the olive oil and turn the heat to medium-high. When the oil is hot, add the seafood and cook until it is half-done, or approximately 2 minutes. The seafood should just be turning opaque on the edges. Add the mushrooms, garlic, basil, and shallots. Sauté the seafood and mushroom mixture for approximately 1 minute longer.

Remove the pan from the heat briefly, add the wine, stir, and return the pan to the heat. Cook the mixture over medium heat for approximately 2 minutes, until the pan juices have been reduced. Add the butter and continue cooking and stirring over medium heat until the butter has melted into the sauce.

To serve this dish family-style, put the noodles on a platter, then pour the seafood and sauce over the noodles. You may want to garnish with a few chopped green onions.

*Courtesy of Aaron Whiting, Uncle Billy's Restaurant*

# MISO BUTTERFISH WITH OSHITASHI

## SERVES 6

4 pounds butterfish, cut into ½-inch thick fillets

Canola oil for sautéing

## MARINADE

½ cup white miso

½ cup mirin

## GREENS

2 pounds leafy greens or zucchini

## GARNISH

Lemon slices

Teriyaki sauce (your favorite brand or your favorite home recipe)

Goma (roasted sesame seeds)

Miyo's, a Japanese restaurant, opened in Waiakea Village in 1988. They are well known for delicious side salads made with fresh, locally grown greens and touched with just a hint of dressing. Their motto is KISS (which I prefer to read as Keep It Simple, Sweetheart). Their dishes are generally simple, but so well made as to be memorable. Their miso butterfish is one of my favorites.

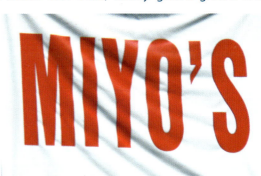

*If you can't find or don't like butterfish, you can substitute any white meat fish, such as black cod, ono, yellowtail, or hamachi. Salmon, while not a white meat fish, also works well in this recipe.*

*The fish is served on a bed of parboiled fresh greens. You can use a variety of greens for this dish: spinach is traditional, but you can substitute bok choy (Chinese cabbage) or whatever is fresh and local. In a pinch, you can use thinly sliced zucchini or carrot.*

Mix the ingredients for the marinade. Put the marinade and the fish fillets in a 1-gallon re-sealable plastic bag and marinate in the refrigerator for at least 6 hours; overnight would be better. Turn the bag occasionally so that all the fillets are well marinated.

**To prepare the greens:** Wash and trim the greens, removing any tough stems. Greens with small leaves, such as spinach, can be left whole. Greens with large leaves should be torn into 2 or 3 pieces. If you are using zucchini or carrot, trim, peel, and then slice the vegetable into thin rounds or long thin strips lengthwise. A kitchen mandolin will help you cut thin slices or strips.

Bring a pot of water to a boil and add the greens or zucchini. Let them cook only for a minute or two, until they are wilted but not mushy. Empty the pot into a large colander to drain the greens. (Careful: don't splash yourself with boiling water.) Then "shock" the greens in ice water for a few minutes. (A bowl full of water and ice cubes will do the trick.) The vegetables should remain green (or orange, if you're using carrots). Again, drain the vegetables in the colander. Cut them into pieces about 1 inch long. Use your hands to squeeze out more of the water.

*To cook the fish:* Heat the canola oil in a large sauté or frying pan over medium-high heat. The oil should be hot enough that when you add the fish to the pan, the fish makes a sizzling sound. Sauté both sides of the fillets. The mixture of miso and mirin will burn easily; that's fine. Just a hint of char adds flavor. Be careful, however, not to over cook.

Don't crowd the pan, or the fish will simmer rather than sear. If you have a smallish pan, you may need to cook the fish in several batches.

*To serve:* If you're serving this restaurant-style, divide the greens between 6 serving plates and nestle the fish and a lemon slice against the greens. Drizzle the fish and greens with teriyaki sauce. Sprinkle the goma on the greens.

If serving family-style, arrange the fish and greens on a large platter, garnish, and let your family help themselves.

*Courtesy of Miyo's*

# TRIPE STEW

MAKES 4–6 SERVINGS

5 pounds tripe, cleaned well, cut into bite-size pieces, approximately ½-inch x 2-inches

2 carrots, peeled, cut into ½-inch pieces

1 green sweet pepper, cut into ½-inch pieces

2 celery stalks, cut into ½-inch pieces

1 round onion, cut into 1-inch cubes

1½ cups tomato sauce

2 teaspoons salt

1½ teaspoons black pepper

1½ teaspoons chili powder

### ROUX

1 tablespoon butter

1 tablespoon all-purpose white flour

## KEN'S HOUSE OF PANCAKES

When Ken's House of Pancakes opened in 1971, some Hilo locals thought Ken Pruitt was lōlō: Hilo was too small to need a 24-hour restaurant. Boy, were they ever wrong! Ken's was soon a popular, late-night hangout as well as a convenient dinner spot for folks working midnight shifts.

Here's one of Ken's signature dishes. Ric Maiava, current owner and manager, says of this recipe: "If you let it cool, refrigerate it overnight, and reheat it for the next day, eh, broke da mouth!"

(As vegetables vary in size, you may want to adjust the vegetable quantities to your taste. However, in a stew like this, it's hard to go wrong.)

Put the tripe in a large stockpot, add water to cover, and cook over medium-heat for 45 minutes. Drain and rinse the tripe. Return the tripe to the stockpot, add water to cover, and cook again. Cook until the tripe is soft. Skim any residue from the surface of the water. If you prefer, you can drain the tripe, cover with water again, and cook for a third time.

Add the carrots, peppers, celery, onions, tomato sauce, salt, black pepper, and chili powder to the tripe and its cooking water. Bring the stew to a boil, then turn down the heat and let the dish simmer for 30-45 minutes, or until all the vegetables are soft enough to eat.

Put a colander over a large bowl; pour the stew into the colander. The solids will stay in the colander, and the soup or sauce will drain into the bowl.

***To make the roux:*** Melt the butter in a sauté pan or skillet over medium heat. When the butter is melted, add the flour. Whisk the roux until it is completely smooth, without any lumps. Cook, whisking, for 3–4 minutes. Do not burn the roux. Some dishes require a dark roux, but this stew needs a plain white roux.

Add a little of the soup or sauce to the roux in the pan, whisking to prevent lumps. Add a little more sauce and whisk. When you have a smooth mixture, empty the contents of the pan into the bowl of soup or sauce, stirring or whisking as you add. The sauce should thicken into a tasty gravy.

Mix the solid ingredients from the stew with the thickened gravy. If the bowl is large enough, and you are planning to serve the stew immediately, you can do this in the bowl. Otherwise, you will want to return the solids and the gravy to the stockpot, stir well, and keep the stew warm until you are ready to serve.

This stew tastes better if you put it in a covered container and refrigerate it overnight. The flavors "marry." Reheat on the stovetop or in a microwave. This soup also freezes well. You may want to freeze it in several smaller portions so that you needn't thaw a large block just to get enough stew for two.

*Courtesy of Ken's House of Pancakes*

# CHAPTER 4

# CELEBRATIONS

IN THE old days, there weren't many fancy "white tablecloth" restaurants on the island. We were mostly working folk, and when we ate out, we ate at restaurants that prepared simple, inexpensive, tasty food. Nothing wrong with that; those are some of my favorite restaurants. But there are times—like a wedding anniversary, a birthday, or when hosting visitors—when you want to celebrate a special occasion in style. There wasn't much choice back then.

Now we have a thriving up-market tourist industry, supporting some world-class restaurants. There are also a number of fine restaurants that serve a sophisticated local clientele. Here are a few of the places I like to go on special occasions. All of them have been gracious enough to share recipes with me (and with you).

# COCONUT CREAM OF CELERY SOUP

### KILAUEA LODGE

The Kilauea Lodge, in Volcano, was once a YMCA retreat center. It still features an "international fireplace of friendship": a large fireplace decorated with stones and coins from all over the world. Now it is a country inn, owned by Lorna and Albert Jeyte.

Dinners open with your choice of Albert's homemade soup or salad. Here is one of his special soups.

*Note that the celery and potatoes can be roughly chopped. As long as the pieces are small enough to purée in a food processor, they're fine.*

**MAKES 8-10 SERVINGS**

10 cups chicken broth
3 pounds celery stalks, cubed
2 pounds russet potatoes, peeled, cubed
2 cups milk
½ cup heavy cream
½ cup coconut syrup
1½ teaspoons celery salt
1 teaspoon white pepper
1 cup (2 sticks) unsalted butter

**GARNISH**
Parsley, finely chopped

Pour the chicken stock into a large (at least 4 quart) pot and bring it to a boil over medium-high heat. Purée the chopped celery and potatoes in food processor until very fine. Add the purée to the boiling chicken broth and beat with a whip for 2 minutes. Add the milk and heavy cream, then the coconut syrup, and stir to mix. Bring the soup to a boil, then reduce the heat to low. Add the celery salt and white pepper; stir. Cover the pot and let the soup simmer for 40 minutes. Stir it frequently.

Remove the pot from the stove. Ladle the soup, bit by bit, into a fine sieve set over a 4-quart bowl. Push the soup through the sieve. After all the soup has been sieved, discard the residue left in the sieve.

Cut the butter into ½-inch pieces and add it to the hot cream of celery soup. Whisk the soup until the butter has dissolved.

**To serve**: Ladle the soup into soup bowls and sprinkle with chopped parsley.

*Courtesy of Kilauea Lodge*

# BAKED STUFFED SHRIMP

**MAKES 8 SERVINGS**

48 large shrimp, butterflied

### CHEESE SAUCE
1½ cups milk

3 cups grated or shredded
   sharp cheese

¼ cup butter

¼ cup flour

Dash of salt

Dash of dry mustard

Dash of white pepper

Dash of Worcestershire sauce

(Here, a dash is approximately
   ¹⁄₁₆ of a teaspoon)

### STUFFING
¾ cup minced onions

¼ cup minced celery

2 tablespoons minced parsley

¼ cup butter

1 tablespoon sherry

¼ pound Dungeness crabmeat

¼ pound white fish, steamed

½ pound bread crumbs

### HOLLANDAISE SAUCE
24 ounces butter (6 sticks)

5 egg yolks, beaten

⅛ teaspoon cayenne pepper

1 tablespoon lemon juice

## JAMESON'S BY THE SEA

Jameson's By the Sea overlooks Magic Sands Beach on the Kona Coast. Great view, great food—a fine place for a celebration. One of my favorite dishes here is the shrimp stuffed with crabmeat and white fish.

*To prepare the cheese sauce:* Heat the butter in a saucepot over medium heat. Mix the flour into the melted butter and whisk until you have a smooth paste (the roux). Add the dry mustard, salt, and pepper to the roux and mix well. Slowly add the milk to the roux, mixing with a whisk the whole time to prevent lumps. As the milk and roux heat, the mixture will thicken. Add the Worcestershire sauce and shredded sharp cheddar cheese. Cook briefly until the cheese melts and remove from heat.

*To prepare the stuffing:* Sauté the minced onions and celery in the butter until tender, then add the parsley and sherry; mix well. In a large mixing bowl, combine the crabmeat, fish, and the cheese sauce. Then tip the onion and celery mixture into the bowl and mix well. Divide the stuffing into 24 equal portions. Form each dab of stuffing into a shrimp-sized wedge.

*To prepare the Hollandaise sauce:* Heat the butter in a heavy saucepan or the top of a double boiler until it is hot and foamy, but not browned.

In a small bowl, whisk or beat egg yolks with the lemon juice and cayenne pepper. Gradually add the butter to the egg yolks, whisking as you pour. Don't add the butter all at once or the eggs will curdle. Return the sauce to the saucepan or double boiler and beat over low heat until the sauce thickens slightly.

*To prepare the shrimp:* Stack shrimp in pairs. Place wedges of stuffing on top of shrimp and place on baking sheet. Bake at 350°F for 5 minutes or until shrimp are cooked.

Serve the stuffed shrimp with the Hollandaise sauce.

*Courtesy of Jameson's By the Sea*

# KONA COFFEE CRUSTED RACK OF LAMB STUFFED WITH PORTOBELLO MUSHROOMS

## MAKES 2 SERVINGS

2 Frenched racks of lamb, approximately 1½ pounds each

### CRUST

½ cup roasted Kona coffee beans, coarsely ground

2 tablespoons Hawaiian 'alaea salt

½ teaspoon ground white pepper

### STUFFING

3 large portobello mushrooms, finely chopped

¼ cup finely diced red pepper

¼ cup finely diced sweet onion

3 tablespoons chopped parsley

1 cup heavy cream

2 tablespoons butter

2 tablespoons olive oil

## SHERATON KEAUHOU

The following recipe won Chef Arnold Arellano of the Sheraton Keauhou second place in the professional division of the 2007 Kona Coffee Festival Recipe Contest.

*The original recipe calls for Frenched rack of lamb. This is a special cut that looks elegant on a restaurant plate. The technique is too elaborate to describe in detail here. If you have never Frenched a rack of lamb, you might ask your butcher to prepare it for you.*

**To make the garnish (optional):** Peel a carrot, then use the carrot peeler to make long strips of carrot. Roll them up and push a toothpick through each roll.

Wash several stalks of green onion; trim off the roots, and then cut off the tops of the onions just where the white is shading into green. The trimmed onion should be some 3 inches long. Holding onto the bottom of the stalk, slice the top lengthwise into long strips, still attached to the stalk.

Put the carrots and the onions into a container full of water and let them chill in the refrigerator. The ends of the onion brush will curl, and the carrots will become delightfully crisp.

**To prepare the stuffing:** Sauté the mushrooms, red pepper, and onions in the butter and olive oil. Add the cream and parsley. Purée the sauce in a blender. Cool it to room temperature. When it is cool, put it in a pastry bag with a ½-inch round tip. Cut slits in the lamb and pipe the stuffing into the lamb.

(continued on page 82)

(continued from page 81)

## SAUCE

2 tablespoons coffee liqueur
½ cup chicken stock
1 tablespoon dry red wine
2 tablespoons unsalted
    butter, chopped

## GARNISH (OPTIONAL)

Carrot curls
Green onion brushes

**To cook the lamb:** Mix the ingredients for the crust and press it into the lamb. Roast the meat at 350°F until done. Rare lamb should reach 140°F, medium 150°F, and well done, 160°F.

**To make the sauce:** Combine the liqueur, stock, and wine and cook over medium heat until the sauce is reduced by half. Add the butter, let it melt, and whisk to finish.

**To serve:** Drizzle the sauce over the rack of lamb. Garnish with fresh carrot curls and green onion brushes.

*Courtesy of Chef Arnold Arellano, Sheraton Keauhou*

A New Departure in the Coffee Business.

CHOICE KONA COFFEE

TRADE MARK.

# GRILLED SHRIMP NACHOS

**MAKES 4 SERVINGS**

### NACHOS

8 man doo wrappers, square

8 jumbo (16/20 per pound) shrimp, peeled and deveined

1 cup shredded smoked mozzarella

1 cup thinly sliced won bok cabbage

1 cup thinly sliced red cabbage

1 cup julienned carrots

½ cup diced tomatoes (¼-inch dice), peeled and deseeded

½ cup corn relish

### CURRY LIME SAUCE

¼ cup bottled tempura sauce

¼ cup strained Thai sweet chili sauce

¼ cup lime juice (juice of 2 limes, approximately)

1 teaspoon sugar

### CAFÉ PESTO

There are two Café Pestos: the original café, in Kawai-hae (opened 1989), and the downtown Hilo café (opened 1992). Both bustle with business, attracting tourists and locals alike. Food critics praise the eclectic menu, which ranges from pizza to upscale entrées.

Here, Chef Casey Halpern shares some unusual shrimp nachos.

*To make the green onion curls:* Trim and wash a few green onion stalks. Cut off the bottom, the roots, and the top, leaving a piece of onion approximately 3½ inches long. With a sharp knife, cut lengthwise through the top half of the stalk, leaving the two halves still attached at the bottom. Roll the stalk 45 degrees and make another lengthwise cut. You'll end up with a green onion "brush." Repeat until you've shredded all the stalks. Put the brushes into a covered container full of water and set it in the refrigerator to chill. The sliced onion ends will crisp and curl.

*To make the curry lime sauce:* Mix together all ingredients and adjust taste with sugar or chili sauce. Makes ½ cup. Use ¼ cup of the sauce for the nachos and refrigerate the rest.

(continued on page 85)

(continued from page 83)

**CILANTRO CRÈME FRAICHE**

¼ cup sour cream
1 tablespoon chopped
   cilantro
1 tablespoon heavy cream
Salt and pepper to taste

**GARNISH**

Toasted sesame seeds
Green onion curls

*To make the cilantro crème fraiche:* Mix all ingredients. Use ¼ cup of the crème fraiche for the nachos and refrigerate the rest.

Cut the man doo wrappers in half, on the diagonal, and prick them with a fork. Fry the man doo halves in vegetable oil heated to 350°F, until both sides are golden brown. Remove the crispy man doo from the oil and lay them out on paper towels to drain and cool.

Season the shrimp with salt and pepper and grill until medium rare, about 3-5 minutes each side. Split the shrimp in half lengthwise.

Pre-heat the oven to 350°F.

Mix the cabbage, carrot, tomato, and corn relish together. Divide the vegetables into 4 equal portions and put one portion in the middle of each of 4 salad plates.

Lay out the 16 man doo chips on a lightly oiled baking pan. Divide the grated smoked mozzarella into 16 portions and top each man doo chip with a portion of cheese. Bake in the 350°F oven until the cheese melts, or about 5 minutes. Watch closely, or you'll burn the chips.

*To serve:* Put four of the cheesy chips atop each serving of salad. Top each of the chips with half a shrimp. Drizzle the curry lime sauce on the vegetables and top the shrimp with a teaspoon of the cilantro crème fraiche. Garnish with sesame seeds and green onion curls.

*Courtesy of Chef Casey Halpern, Café Pesto*

# WOK CHARRED 'AHI OVER SLAW

2 sashimi-style cuts of 'ahi,
approximately 4 ounces each

## MARINADE

½ cup oil

2 teaspoons chopped shallots

2 teaspoons grated fresh ginger

2 teaspoons crushed garlic

1 teaspoon dried thyme

1 teaspoon dried marjoram

2 teaspoons crushed dried chilies
or ½ teaspoon cayenne

½ teaspoon salt

1 tablespoon lemon juice (juice
from ½ lemon, approximately)

## SLAW

1½ cups thinly sliced Chinese
cabbage

½ cup mung bean sprouts

½ cup thinly sliced Bermuda
onion

¼ cup chopped cilantro

## DIPPING SAUCE

2 tablespoons wasabi powder

2 tablespoons water

2 cups soy sauce

½ cup fresh lemon juice

⅓ cup mirin

## MERRIMEN'S

In 1988 Peter Merrimen opened Merrimen's in Waimea. From the beginning, Peter has cultivated a personal relationship with local farmers and ranchers, encouraging them to grow produce for his restaurant, including new varieties of vegetables and fruits. Peter is one of the founding fathers of Hawai'i Regional Cuisine.

*To prepare the marinade:* Mix together all the ingredients for the marinade.

*To prepare the slaw:* Mix all ingredients and chill.

*To prepare the dipping sauce:* Make a thick paste with water and wasabi powder. Add the soy sauce, lemon juice, and mirin, and mix well.

*To prepare the fish:* Roll the 'ahi in the marinade. Sear the 'ahi in a hot wok or hot skillet for 30 seconds on each side.

*To serve:* Slice the 'ahi and serve it on a bed of slaw, with a dish of dipping sauce on the side.

*Courtesy of Merrimen's*

# KONA COFFEE ALMOND 'SMORE TORTE WITH COCOA NIB TUILES

**MAKES A 9 X 13-INCH TORTE**

### GRAHAM CRUST FOR 'SMORES (BOTTOM LAYER)

1 pound graham crackers

5 ounces sugar

9 ounces butter, melted

### SAINT MARK'S ALMOND CAKE (SECOND LAYER)

11 ounces sugar

6½ ounces almond meal

3½ ounces cake flour, sifted

11 ounces egg whites

6½ ounces sugar

### MOCHA GANACHE (THIRD LAYER)

8 ounces bittersweet chocolate

8 ounces milk chocolate

1 teaspoon Kona Coffee, finely ground (use a sieve to sift out any large pieces)

1 cup heavy cream

## MAUNA LANI RESORT

The resort's pastry chef, Kathy Solywoda, submitted this recipe and won first place in the 2007 Kona Coffee Cultural Festival Recipe Contest in the Professional Dessert division.

*To make the graham crust (bottom layer):* Preheat the oven to 375°F. Combine all ingredients. Press the mixture firmly into a 9 x 13-inch pan. Bake the crust for 10 minutes. Set aside to cool.

*To make the almond cake (second layer):* Lightly grease a 9 x 13-inch pan. Preheat the oven to 350°F.

Whisk together the first three ingredients. Whip the egg whites and remaining sugar until the meringue forms soft peaks. Gently fold the flour mixture into the whites.

Bake the almond cake for 12 minutes. Cool slightly, then unmold the cake onto the graham crust.

*To make the mocha ganache (third layer):* Bring the heavy cream to a boil; pour it over the chocolate and coffee. When the chocolate has melted, stir the mixture to remove all lumps. Pour the ganache onto the almond cake layer.

## COFFEE MARSHMALLOW (TOP LAYER)

½ ounce gelatin

½ cup water

2 cups sugar

¾ cup corn syrup

¼ cup water

2 teaspoons Kona coffee reduction or extract

1 teaspoon Kona coffee, finely ground

¼ teaspoon salt

## COCOA NIB TUILE (GARNISH)

2 ounces powdered sugar

2 ounces butter, softened

2 ounces corn syrup

1 ounce pastry or all-purpose flour

2 ounces cocoa nibs

**To make the coffee marshmallow (top layer):** Bloom the gelatin in ½ cup water in a mixing bowl. Combine the sugar, corn syrup, and ¼ cup water in a saucepan and bring to a boil. Allow to boil for 1 minute. Pour the syrup directly over gelatin and whip for about 10 minutes. (This is best done with a heavy-duty stand mixer equipped with a whip.) Add the last three ingredients towards the end of whipping time. Pour over the cooled ganache layer.

**To make the cocoa nib tuile (garnish):** Combine the powdered sugar and softened butter with a paddle beater or a wooden spoon until you have a smooth mixture. Add the corn syrup, flour, and coffee nibs, mixing after each ingredient is added. Roll dough into a 3-inch-diameter log. Wrap the dough in parchment or waxed paper and chill. Once it is solid, cut it into ¼-inch-thick slices and bake on a Silpat mat at 350°F for 5–7 minutes.

**To serve**: Arrange the tuiles on top of the cake.

*Courtesy of Chef Kathy Solywoda, Mauna Lani Resort*

# MACADAMIA NUT PRALINE SEARED SCALLOPS

**MAKES 4 SERVINGS**

20 jumbo (U10) scallops
¼ cup macadamia nuts
2 tablespoons brown sugar
Pinch red chili flakes
High-temperature vegetable
    cooking spray

**NOODLES**

12 ounces angel hair pasta or
    somen noodles
4 tablespoons butter
Salt and pepper to taste

**BEURRE BLANC**

¼ cup heavy cream
½ pound unsalted butter
2 shallots
½ cup white wine
Salt and pepper to taste

**GARNISH**

⅔ cup micro greens (tender
    baby greens) or other
    delicate greens, such
    as pea shoots or baby
    arugula

## HILO BAY CAFÉ

The Hilo Bay Café opened in 2003. Owner Kim Snaggerud and Chef Joshua Ketner serve contemporary American cuisine. Whenever possible they buy organic produce from local farms, such as Kekela Farms and Mother Nature's Miracle Farms.

Chef Josh shared this recipe for scallops.

Finely chop the macadamia nuts, or pulse in a food processor until finely chopped. Add the sugar and chili flakes to the nuts and mix well.

Prepare the pasta or somen noodles as directed on the package. Set aside.

Sauté the bacon until it is crispy, crumble it, and set aside.

***To make the beurre blanc sauce:*** Simmer the white wine and shallots in a medium-size saucepan over medium heat. Cook until the wine is reduced by half. Add the heavy cream and again reduce by half.

Add the butter one tablespoon at a time, stirring constantly, until it has melted into the sauce. Add salt and pepper to taste. Strain mixture through a fine sieve mesh and set aside.

**To brown the pasta or somen:** Brown 4 tablespoons of butter over medium-high heat until the butter foams and just starts to brown. Add the noodles and toss to heat. Remove the noodles from the heat.

**To prepare the scallops:** Preheat broiler to medium-high. Coat an oven-proof sauté pan or skillet with high-temperature vegetable spray.

Heat the sauté pan over medium-high heat. Salt and pepper the scallops, then add them to the sauté pan and sear on one side for 2 minutes. Turn them over and then remove from heat. The residual heat in the pan will cook the other side of the scallops.

Sprinkle the scallops with the macadamia nut mixture. Put the pan full of scallops under the broiler; broil until the sugar in the macadamia nut mixture caramelizes. This should only take some 30 seconds. Watch the scallops carefully so that they do not overcook. If they do, they will be tough.

**To assemble:** Put a portion of the browned noodles in the center of each plate. Drizzle beurre blanc around the noodles. Place five scallops on the beurre blanc. Garnish with bacon and micro greens.

*Courtesy of Chef Joshua Ketner, Hilo Bay Café*

# BANANA BREAD

**MAKES 2 LARGE LOAVES**

4 cups mashed bananas
  (approximately 7½ large
  bananas)
2½ cups sugar
1¼ cup vegetable oil
3 medium eggs
1 teaspoon Hawaiian vanilla
  extract
4½ cups bread flour
½ teaspoon baking powder
2 teaspoon baking soda
1 teaspoon salt

## MAUNA KEA BEACH HOTEL

The Mauna Kea Beach Hotel was a popular place for Sunday brunch until it was heavily damaged in the 2006 earthquake and forced to close. It will reopen after two years of renovation.

Executive Chef Piet Wigmans gave me this banana bread recipe.

Preheat oven to 350°F. Grease and flour two loaf pans.

Sift together the flour, baking powder, soda, and salt.

Put the mashed bananas in your mixer bowl. Add the sugar, oil, eggs, and vanilla extract to the bananas and mix for 5 minutes. Gradually add the sifted flour, baking powder, baking soda, and salt; mix well.

Bake for 45 minutes to 1 hour, or until a toothpick inserted into the center of the loaf comes out clean.

*Courtesy of Chef Piet Wigmans, Mauna Kea Beach Hotel*

# SEARED ISLAND KAMPACHI WITH KAMUELA TOMATO POKE & TOASTED GARLIC VINAIGRETTE

### ICHIBAN DASHI
**MAKES 5 CUPS**

6-inch piece of dashi kombu
1 cup katsuoboshi (shaved
    bonito)
4 cups water

### PONZU SAUCE
**MAKES ¾ CUP**

⅓ cup soy sauce
¼ cup fresh lemon juice
1 tablespoon rice wine
    vinegar
⅓ cup ichiban dashi

### KAMUELA TOMATO POKE
**MAKES 4 CUPS**

4 Kamuela tomatoes
    (approximately 1 pound)
¼ teaspoon chili flakes
1 teaspoon inamona
    (crushed kukui nuts)
2 teaspoons red Hawaiian
    salt
¼ cup green onion, chopped
1 tablespoon sesame oil
¼ cup red onion, chopped

## COAST GRILLE

The Coast Grille at the Hapuna Beach Prince Hotel is one of my favorite places to celebrate a special occasion. Chef Brett Villarmia shared these wonderful dishes, which use local ingredients.

*Here's a fancy looking dish that will actually be easy to prepare if you've made the following recipes.*

## ICHIBAN DASHI

*Use this fresh dashi to make ponzu sauce or as a soup base with miso. You can find all the necessary ingredients in any Oriental grocery section.*

## PONZU SAUCE

Mix and refrigerate until ready to use.

## KAMUELA TOMATO POKE

*You can serve this poke with the kampachi recipe that follows. It is also a fine accompaniment to other meat and fish dishes.*

If you like a wet poke, don't remove the seeds from the tomatoes. If you like your poke drier, halve or quarter the tomatoes and remove the seeds. Cut the tomatoes into ¼-inch cubes and put them in a medium-size mixing bowl. Add the rest of the ingredients; let tomatoes marinate for 30 minutes. Drain the tomato poke in a colander and set aside until ready to serve. If the poke is prepared more than an hour ahead of time, refrigerate the poke.

(continued on page 95)

(continued from page 94)

**TOASTED GARLIC
VINAIGRETTE
MAKES 1 CUP**

4 ounces canola oil

1 ounce garlic, minced

1 ounce soy sauce

4 ounces ponzu (Japanese
   citrus sauce; see recipe
   above)

**SEARED ISLAND KAMPACHI
MAKES 4 SERVINGS**

8 ounces Kona kampachi
   sashimi

Salt and pepper to taste

2–3 tablespoons canola oil

**GARNISH**

2 ounces crispy won ton
   strips (you can use ONE
   TON Chips by Maebo)

8 ounces tomato poke

4 tablespoons toasted garlic
   vinaigrette

¼ cup fresh cilantro leaves

# TOASTED GARLIC VINAIGRETTE

*You can use this vinaigrette in the kampachi recipe that follows. It also goes well with other fried fish dishes.*

Put the oil and garlic in a small saucepot; heat the pot over medium heat. Cook until the garlic is toasted but not burnt, or about 2 minutes. Add the soy sauce and ponzu to the pot; this will prevent the garlic from cooking any further. Remove from the heat and chill until ready to use.

# SEARED ISLAND KAMPACHI

Season the kampachi with salt and pepper. Put the canola oil in a sauté pan and heat it over medium-high heat. When the oil is hot, add the fish and sear for 5 seconds on each side. Chill the seared fish in the refrigerator until you are ready to slice and serve it.

***To serve***: Put the tomato poke in the center of a serving plate. Arrange the won ton strips on the poke. Cut the seared kampachi into thin sashimi slices and drape them over the won ton strips. Drizzle garlic vinaigrette around tomato poke. Garnish with cilantro leaves.

*Courtesy of Chef Brett Villarmia, Coast Grille*

# PURPLE SWEET POTATO CHEESECAKE WITH HAUPIA TOPPING

**MAKES ONE 9-INCH CHEESECAKE**

### CRUST

¾ cup macadamia nuts, finely chopped

¾ cup graham cracker crumbs

½ cup melted butter

### CHEESECAKE

1½ cups steamed and mashed Okinawa purple sweet potatoes (takes approximately 2 potatoes)

1 pound cream cheese (two 8 ounce packages)

3 large eggs

¾ cup sugar

1 teaspoon vanilla extract

### HAUPIA

2 cups coconut milk

1 cup sugar

2 cups water

½ cup cornstarch

### HILO HAWAIIAN HOTEL

The Hilo Hawaiian Hotel shared this onolicious cheesecake recipe. Made with local sweet potatoes and coconut milk, it's as local as local can be.

**To prepare the crust:** Preheat oven to 350°F. Mix all ingredients. Pat the crust into a 9-inch spring form pan. Bake for 10 minutes in 350°F oven. Remove the pan from the oven, but leave the oven on.

**To prepare the cheesecake:** Put the mashed sweet potato, cream cheese, eggs, sugar, and vanilla in a mixer bowl and beat until well blended. Pour the cheesecake batter over the crust in the spring form pan. Bake for 1 hour in the 350°F oven. Cool completely.

**To prepare the haupia:** Mix together the coconut milk, sugar, water, and cornstarch in a heavy saucepan. Cook over low heat, stirring constantly, until the haupia thickens.

**To assemble:** Spread the warm haupia evenly over the top of the cheesecake.

*Courtesy of Hilo Hawaiian Hotel*

# CHAPTER 5

# GONE BUT NOT FORGOTTEN

**IF** you grew up on the Big Island, you probably have fond memories of some great restaurants that are no longer with us. Here are a few recipes that may remind you of the good old days.

The Goya family, courtesy of Ramon Goya.

## Historical Background of May's Fountain and Goya Bros.

The Goya Bros. Service Station, Grocery Store and Ellen's Liquor Store on Kamehameha Avenue was founded in June, 1933 by Aizo and Haruko Goya, their two sons, Ronald (Square) and Richard (Hick) and daughter, Mrs. Ellen Hiroko Ivey. In 1942, the Goya Bros. U-Drive and Taxi Service was added to the business.

The April 1, 1946 tsunami severely damaged the business and it was rebuilt at the same site. The new business was then changed to May's Fountain.

The May, 1960 tsunami again wiped out the business. In July, 1960, the Goya Taxi - May's Deli and Liquor Store relocated to the corner of Ponahawai and Punahoa Street.

On December 15, 1977, Ronald and May retired the business.

# CORNED BEEF HASH, HILO STYLE

**MAKES 8 TO 10 SERVINGS**

6 large, smooth baking
potatoes (approximately
6 pounds)

**MASHED POTATOES**
2 tablespoons butter
½ cup whole milk

**FILLING**
2 cups chopped corned beef
or other cold meat
2 tablespoons grated onion
¾ cup grated cheese
Salt, pepper, and paprika to
taste

## OLA'A STEAK HOUSE

Yasuo and Aiko Ogata opened the Ola'a Steak House just four days before Pearl Harbor was attacked in 1941. They had received enough rice as grand opening gifts to allow them to stay open. Eventually, many soldiers were stationed on the Big Island, and they kept the Ogatas busy. The Ogatas sold their business and retired in the late 1960s. The lucky folks who got to eat there will always remember their specialties: steak with rice, hamburger steak, corned beef hash, shrimp curry, pork chops, and Italian meatballs. The food was good and cooked with care.

*Here is a recipe for corned beef hash. It's not the Ogatas' recipe, but it's close.*

Bake the potatoes until they are soft. Cut them in half lengthwise. Remove the cooked potato meat from the skins. Do this carefully; you want to keep the skins whole.

Put the potato meat in a bowl and add butter, salt, pepper, and milk to taste. Mash the potatoes until fluffy.

Fill the potato skins with chopped corned beef mixed with onion. Sprinkle the cheese and paprika over the meat. Bake until browned in a 400°F oven.

Serve the baked corned beef with a side of mashed potatoes.

# OLD STYLE SAIMIN

**MAKES 6 SERVINGS**

Saimin noodles
Sliced kamaboko
Omelet shreds
Sliced green onions

### BROTH
1 (10-inch) section of pig foot
1 gallon water
1 cup packed dried
    katsuoboshi
1 (3 x 6-inch) piece dashi
    kombu
1 carrot, cut into large pieces
1 celery stalk, cut into large
    pieces
3 aburage, cut into large
    pieces
Shrimp shells, if available
6 shiitake mushrooms
¼ cup soy sauce
1 tablespoon salt

## KK'S PLACE

Kiyomi and Fumie Kobata opened KK's Place in 1950. It was the best place on the island for saimin.

Their saimin dashi (soup stock) was unforgettable. Pigs' feet, shrimp shells, katsuoboshi, dashi kombu, and carrots were simmered for a very long time to bring out the best of each ingredient. No MSG or instant packaged dashi was used. Mrs. Kobata remembers buying cases of pigs' feet weekly for her saimin stock.

***To prepare the broth:*** Boil all ingredients together in large stock pot. After 15 minutes, remove the dashi kombu. Continue boiling, then lower heat and simmer for 1-2 hours. When broth is needed, ladle it from the top, leaving all the solid ingredients behind.

Cook the saimin according to package instructions. Place noodles in bowl, top with sliced kamaboko, julienned omelet, and green onions. Pour broth over the noodles, enough to cover.

Note that quantities are given loosely here. How much kamaboko and omelet to add to the noodles is up to you. If you need directions for making the omelet shreds, see page 5.

*Courtesy of KK's Place*

# BI BIM BAP

## MAKES 4 SERVINGS

1 pound thin sliced beef, sliced
    thinly as for teriyaki
½ bunch watercress
½ package bean sprouts
1 small zucchini
1 small cucumber
¼ package warabi or fern shoots
1 small carrot
4 eggs
2 cups hot rice

## VEGETABLE SEASONINGS

Sesame oil
Roasted sesame seeds
Soy sauce
Garlic cloves (or mashed garlic in
    jars, if you're pressed for time)

## SERVE ON THE SIDE

1 bottle Kochujung sauce

## MARINADE

½ cup soy sauce
½ cup brown sugar, honey, or
    granulated sugar
¼ cup roasted sesame seeds
½ cup sesame seed oil
½ cup chopped green onions
⅓ cup (finely minced or crushed)
    freshly peeled garlic

## KAY'S LUNCH CENTER

Owners Allan and Kay Okuda opened Kay's Lunch Center in 1983. They were known for their crispy Korean chicken, Korean barbecued beef, and cream cheese pies. They also served okazushi: a sushi roll full of barbecued meat and takuan strips. Kay's closed its doors in 2005. Here is one of Kay's favorite recipes.

*Kay called this dish the Korean loco moco. It looks complicated, but it is fairly easy if you ordinarily eat Korean food. The vegetables are just the kind of side dishes served with every meal. If you have a refrigerator full of vegetable leftovers, all you need to do is cook rice in the rice cooker, grill some meat, and cook a few eggs over easy.*

**To prepare the barbecued beef:** Mix all the ingredients for the marinade. Marinate the meat slices overnight. I like to do this in a 1-gallon re-sealable plastic bag. Just turn the bag occasionally so that the meat marinates evenly.

Grill the meat over charcoal, about 3-4 minutes on each side. Slice into thin strips.

**To prepare the vegetables:**
**Watercress:** Wash, boil for 4 minutes, squeeze out as much water as you can, cut into 3-inch long pieces.

**Bean sprouts:** Boil in lightly salted water for 2-3 minutes, drain, and cool. Mix with 1 teaspoon sesame oil, 1 tablespoon sesame seeds, and 1 clove of garlic, minced.

**Zucchini:** Wash, slice, boil in lightly salted water, drain, cool, mix with 1 teaspoon sesame oil, 1 tablespoon sesame seeds, and 2 cloves of garlic, minced.

**Cucumber:** Wash, cut lengthwise, slice thinly.

*Courtesy of Kay Okuda*

*Warabi or fern shoots:* Soak in water until plump, drain, sauté in 1 tablespoon oil, 3 tablespoons soy sauce, and 1 minced garlic clove.

*Carrot:* Wash, peel, and shred. Boil in lightly salted water for 1-2 minutes, drain, and cool. Mix with 1 teaspoon sesame oil, 1 tablespoon sesame seeds, and 1 minced garlic clove.

*To assemble:* Set out 4 large bowls. Put ½ cup rice in each bowl. Arrange the vegetables on top of the rice in a decorative circle. Add the grilled beef strips. Top each bowl with one overeasy egg. Serve with Kochujung sauce on the side.

*Note:* After adding Kochujung, mix everything in the bowl together. You should end up with a reddish, delicious mess—dig in!

# RELIABLE WHITE CAKE

**MAKES ONE 9-INCH-DIAMETER CAKE**

3 cups cake flour

3 teaspoons baking powder

¼ teaspoon salt

½ cup butter

1½ cups sugar

2 eggs

1 ⅓ cups milk

1 teaspoon vanilla extract

## ORANGE BUTTER FROSTING

¼ cup orange juice

2 teaspoons lemon juice

1 tablespoon grated orange rind (the rind from 1 orange, approximately)

1 teaspoon grated lemon rind (the rind from ½ lemon, approximately)

3 cups powdered sugar

1 egg yolk

3 tablespoons butter, softened

¼ teaspoon salt

## HILO DRUG AND FOUNTAIN

Hilo Drug and Fountain opened in 1895. Regulars ate lunch specials such as beef stew, nishime, and pork chops, or came for coffee and a piece of cake or pie. The restaurant closed in 1970.

*This old-fashioned white cake with orange butter frosting is typical of the 1940s. A cake like this would probably have been served at Hilo Drug and Fountain.*

**To make the cake:** Measure flour after sifting. Add baking powder and salt and sift three times. Cream butter and sugar until light and fluffy. Add slightly beaten eggs and beat well. Add flour alternately with milk, a little at a time, beating well after each addition. Add vanilla. Bake in two 9-inch round cake pans in a 375°F oven for 25 minutes.

If you'd like to make a four-layer cake, you can cut the baked and cooled layers in half with a strong thread. You can measure, then insert some toothpicks into the side of the layer to mark the cutting line if you're worried about making an even cut.

**To make the frosting:** Combine the juice and grated rind from the orange and lemon; let the mixture stand for 1 minute.

Combine the powdered sugar, egg yolk, butter, and salt. Mix well. Thin the frosting with some of the juice. If you'd like, you can add a little of the grated rind to the frosting now. Beat the frosting until it is smooth. Spread it between the cake layers, then on the top and sides of the cooled cake. If you'd like, you can sprinkle some of the orange and lemon rind on top as a decorative touch.

# KAU YUK OR CHINESE ROAST PORK WITH TARO

**MAKES 8 SERVINGS**

4 pounds belly pork

2 cups peeled, washed, sliced Chinese taro (approximately 2 corms)

2 tablespoons thick or black soy sauce

2 tablespoons regular soy sauce

8 drops red food coloring

½ teaspoon Chinese five-spice

1 star anise

4 tablespoons red bean curd

4 tablespoons brown sugar

2 (½-inch thick) slices of ginger, crushed

2 cloves garlic, crushed

2 teaspoons salt

¼ cup Chinese parsley leaves, for garnish

## SUN SUN LAU

Hilo's Sun Sun Lau first opened in 1939 as a grocery store. They moved from their original building on Keawe Street to Kamehameha Avenue, then to a building by Wailoa Pond, then to their new, large restaurant on Kino'ole. That restaurant was a favorite spot for family gatherings. Many Big Islanders have great memories of weddings and celebrations held at Sun Sun Lau. The Waiakea Lions Club met there weekly. Most of the employees had worked there for years. It was a sad day in Hilo when Sun Sun Lau closed its doors.

*You'll need to handle some fresh taro for this recipe. As Island cooks know, raw taro can irritate your hands (or your mouth, if you make the mistake of eating some). You can wash the taro, and your hands, frequently, or you can wear rubber gloves. Cooked taro is, of course, both safe and delicious.*

**To prepare the pork:** Bring a large pot of water to a boil over high heat. Boil the pork for 5 minutes. Remove the pork and run it under cold water from the faucet. Wipe the pork to dry it. Rub the surface of the pork with thick soy sauce. Fry it in hot oil until it is brown on all sides. Again, put it under cold running water—this time for 3 minutes. Wipe the pork dry and slice it cross-wise into ¼-inch pieces.

Cut the taro into ½-inch-thick slices.

Mix the soy sauce, food coloring, five-spice, star anise, bean curd, brown sugar, ginger, garlic, and salt. Put the pork into this seasoning and allow it to stand for a few minutes.

**To steam:** Place the seasoned pork in a large bowl, skin side down. Arrange the taro slices between the pork slices. Put in a steamer and steam for 2 hours, or until very tender.

**To serve:** Invert the contents of the bowl onto a serving platter. Garnish with Chinese parsley.

# SUMMER 'AHI TARTARE

MAKES 6 SERVINGS

1 pound very fresh 'ahi or
   yellowfin tuna

¼ cup minced sweet onion

2½ tablespoons lemon
   juice (juice of 1 lemon,
   approximately)

2 tablespoons chopped
   cilantro

1 tablespoon minced fresh
   ginger

1 tablespoon soy sauce

1 teaspoon olive oil

1 teaspoon sesame oil

1½ teaspoons grated fresh
   horseradish

½ teaspoon prepared stone-
   ground mustard

Pinch of red chili pepper
   flakes

Salt and white pepper to
   taste

## SAM CHOY'S KALOKO RESTAURANT

Sam Choy and his sister, Claire Wai Sun Choy, opened the Kaloko Restaurant in 1991. It was a favorite with both locals and tourists.

Fresh-caught fish was always available at the Kaloko. The restaurant sold one thousand pounds of fried marlin poke every week. They also sold mahimahi lū'au, steamed opah, weke 'ula, and 'ōpakapaka.

When the cooks cleaned the 'ahi and cut fillets, they scraped the bones to make this 'ahi tartare.

Cut the 'ahi into 1-inch cubes. Combine all ingredients in a food processor and do 6 short pulses until the fish reaches the texture you prefer. Do NOT purée the mixture.

If you don't have a processor, use a sharp knife to mince the 'ahi into ¼-inch cubes. Combine the chopped 'ahi with the other ingredients.

Serve with toast points, crackers, or field greens.

*Courtesy of Chef Sam Choy*

# INARIZUSHI OR CONE SUSHI

MAKES 24 LARGE TRIANGLE
SUSHI OR 40 SMALL
RECTANGLE SUSHI

12 large triangle aburage
   or 20 small rectangle
   aburage
3½ cups rice

### SEASONING FOR ABURAGE

1 cup water
¾ teaspoon salt
1 (1.4 ounce) package dashi-
   no-moto (without MSG)
2 tablespoons soy sauce
6 tablespoons brown sugar

### AWASE-ZU OR VINEGAR MIXTURE

⅔ cup sugar
1½ teaspoons salt
½ cup rice vinegar

### DICED VEGETABLES OR GU FOR THE SUSHI RICE

2 medium carrots, finely
   diced
8 shiitake mushrooms,
   soaked to soften if using
   dry, finely diced
3 ounces (½ block)
   kamaboko, finely diced

## MIZOGUCHI STORE

Mizoguchi Store, on Kamehameha Avenue, made the best cone sushi. Everyone went there to get take-out sushi. The aburage (fried tofu) was seasoned to perfection with soy sauce and brown sugar, and there were bits of carrot and shiitake mushroom in the rice.

*I don't have the authentic Mizoguchi recipe, but the following recipe comes very close.*

**To prepare the aburage:** Cut the aburage triangles or squares in half. Open carefully; you must not tear them.

Boil the aburage in water to cover for 1 hour, or until soft. Drain the cooking water from the pot, then add the seasoning mixture (water, salt, dashi-no-moto, soy sauce, brown sugar) to the aburage. Cook the aburage over medium heat for 10 minutes.

Put a colander over a bowl. Empty the pot into the colander. The aburage will stay in the colander while the cooking liquid drains into the bowl. Save the liquid, as you will use it to cook the carrots, mushrooms, and kamaboko.

**To cook the rice:** Start the rice cooking in the rice cooker.

**To prepare the vegetables and kamaboko:** Pour the aburage cooking liquid into a saucepan; add carrots, mushrooms, and kamaboko. Cook for 10 minutes, or until the carrots are just cooked, but not mushy. Drain the vegetables and kamaboko and set aside.

**To prepare the sushi rice:** Put the hot, cooked rice into a large, shallow container. Mix in the awase-zu, or seasoned vinegar. Mix slowly, a bit at a time, until all the rice is mixed. Add the cooked carrots, mushrooms, and kamaboko to the rice. Mix to combine.

**To assemble the inarizushi:** Fill the warm aburage wrappers loosely with the warm rice mixture. Do not pack the rice tightly.

# TEA CAKES

**MAKES 16
(2 X 2-INCH) TEA CAKES**

6 large eggs, separated
½ teaspoon cream of tartar
¾ cup + 1 cup sugar
1 cup butter, softened
2 cups sifted cake flour
½ teaspoon baking powder
½ teaspoon salt

**ICING**

2 cups powdered sugar
½ cup water
1 tablespoon corn syrup
1 teaspoon almond extract
¼ cup sliced almonds

## ROBERT'S BAKERY

Robert's Bakery was first opened by Robert Taira in the 1950s. When he moved to O'ahu to open King's Bakery, he sold the business to the Hatada brothers, who also ran the Hatada Bakery (which closed in 1994).

The Hatadas made bread and hamburger and hot dog buns; later they added pastries, cakes, and pies to their line. Their tea cakes were my special delight.

*I was unable to get the original recipe, but I've experimented until I can truthfully say that the following recipe comes close.*

Preheat the oven to 350°F. Grease a 9-inch-square cake pan, line it with parchment paper, and grease the parchment paper. Sift together the flour, baking powder, and salt. Beat the egg whites and cream of tartar until soft peaks form. Add ¾ cup sugar gradually, beating until the meringue is very stiff.

In another bowl, using clean beaters, cream the butter and remaining 1 cup of sugar. Add the egg yolks and beat until the mixture is thick and fluffy. Add the sifted dry ingredients in three installments, mixing after each addition. Gently fold the egg whites into the cake batter. Pour the batter into the prepared pan. Bake 50-60 minutes, or until an inserted wooden pick comes out clean. Cool.

**To prepare the icing:** Combine the powdered sugar, water, and corn syrup in a saucepan and cook over medium-low heat, stirring constantly, until mixture thickens. Stir in the almond extract.

**To assemble the tea cakes:** Cut the cake into 2-inch-square pieces with a serrated knife. Carefully remove the cakes from the parchment paper. Place the pieces on a wire rack and slide a cookie sheet underneath. Pour the icing over the tops and sides of the tea cakes. You can touch up the sides with a spatula or butter knife. Any icing that pools on the cookie sheet can be scraped up and poured over the cakes again. While the frosting is still warm, sprinkle the tops of the tea cakes with almonds.

# CANDIED POPCORN

MAKES 8 SERVINGS

¼ cup sugar
10 drops food coloring
3 tablespoons canola oil
½ cup popcorn

## KRESS STORE

The Kress Store, on Kamehameha Avenue in Hilo, was a popular five-and-dime store. There was a popcorn machine in the front of the entrance that made the most 'ono sweet, colored popcorn. A bag cost only ten cents.

*This recipe for candied popcorn reminds me of those 'onolicious bags from the Kress Store.*

Put the sugar and food coloring in a mixing bowl, and blend to color the sugar.

Put the oil in a large pot with a cover. Add one or two kernels of popcorn. Turn the heat to medium-high. When one or more of the kernels pop, you know that the oil is hot enough.

Put the rest of the popcorn into the pot; swirl the pot to coat the kernels with oil. Sprinkle the colored sugar over the popcorn, then cover the pot. When the popcorn starts to pop, shake the pot vigorously to coat the popcorn with sugar and to prevent the sugar from burning.

When the popcorn stops making popping sounds, it's done. Pour it into a large bowl and sprinkle it with ¼ teaspoon salt.

# TERIYAKI BEEF

**MAKES 6 SERVINGS**

1½ pounds teriyaki meat,
   sliced very thin

**MARINADE**

1¼ cups brown or white
   sugar

1¼ cups soy sauce

1 tablespoon salad oil

1 clove garlic, crushed

2 teaspoons crushed ginger

## MAY'S FOUNTAIN

May Goya started her restaurant, May's Fountain, after the tsunami of 1946. The restaurant was destroyed in the tsunami of 1960, and May re-opened on the corner of Ponahawai and Punahoa streets. This popular lunch spot closed in 1977.

*Here is May's recipe for teriyaki beef.*

Mix soy sauce, sugar, oil, garlic, and ginger in a bowl. Add the beef, soak overnight. Charcoal grill or pan fry. When pan frying, cook until the sauce gets thick.

*Courtesy of May Goya*

The Grand Opening of May's Fountain in 1946, courtesy of Ramon Goya.

# MAHIMAHI FLORENTINE

6 (8 ounce) skinned
   mahimahi fillets
1½ teaspoons salt
¾ teaspoon white pepper
1 cup thinly sliced
   onion (1 large onion,
   approximately)
4 tablespoons butter
½ cup dry white wine
3 pounds fresh spinach,
   washed, stemmed, and
   patted dry
A sprinkle of sweet paprika
Lemon wedges for garnish

## MORNAY SAUCE

4 tablespoons butter
4 tablespoons flour
2 cups milk
½ teaspoon salt
¼ teaspoon white pepper
1 teaspoon Worcestershire
   sauce
⅓ cup freshly grated
   Parmesan cheese

## DOTTY'S COFFEE SHOP

Dotty's Coffee Shop opened at the Puainako Town Center in 1984 and closed in 2004 at the Prince Kuhio Plaza. It was a popular place, with many regulars, offering a good meal at an affordable price.

*Here is a wonderful mahimahi dish from Rey Frasco, Dotty's chef and owner. It's a great way to make kids eat their spinach.*

Dotty Frasco, courtesy of Rey Frasco.

Preheat the oven to 350°F. Season the fish with a mixture of 1 teaspoon salt and ½ teaspoon white pepper. Lay the onion slices in the bottom of a large, shallow, buttered baking dish. Arrange the seasoned mahimahi on top. Sprinkle the fish with paprika. Melt 2 tablespoons butter; pour the butter and wine over fish. Bake in the preheated oven for approximately 25 minutes, or until the fish is just cooked.

While the fish is baking, or even several hours beforehand, prepare the Mornay sauce.

**To make the Mornay sauce:** Melt the butter over medium heat in a heavy saucepan. Add the flour. Cook, stirring constantly with a wire whisk, for 4-5 minutes. Slowly pour in the milk, continuing to stir; this will prevent lumps. Simmer the sauce for 20-25 minutes, stirring occasionally to prevent scorching. Season with salt and pepper. Add the Worcestershire sauce and the grated cheese. Simmer 5 minutes longer, stirring frequently.

**To prepare the spinach:** Just before the fish is to be taken out of the oven, prepare the bed of spinach on which the fish will be served. Put the remaining 2 tablespoons of butter in a deep pot. Add the spinach, ½ teaspoon salt, and ¼ teaspoon white pepper. Cover the pot and cook over medium heat, stirring occasionally, until the spinach has wilted and turned tender.

**To serve:** When the fish is done, place the wilted spinach on a warm platter. Arrange the fish on top of the spinach. Scatter the sliced onions over the fish and coat with the Mornay sauce. Garnish with lemon wedges.

*Courtesy of Rey Frasco, Dotty's Coffee Shop*

# HARD TACK

MAKES 24 CRACKERS

1½ cups milk

4 cups flour

4 tablespoons butter,
    softened

1 tablespoon brown sugar

1½ teaspoons salt

## HILO MACARONI COMPANY

The Hilo Macaroni Company manufactured these crackers in Hilo from 1917 to 2003. Generations of Hawai'i residents grew up eating these crackers. Many tears were shed when the Hilo Macaroni Company closed.

The crackers are a local version of hard tack, the long-lasting crackers that were common fare on sailing ships for centuries. Hard tack was baked and packed into barrels, where it could last for years.

It is said that a German ship was stuck in Hilo Harbor and ran out of hard tack. They taught a few Hilo bakers—including Mr. Ikeda, of Hilo Macaroni—how to make hard tack so that they could re-supply.

The Hilo Macaroni Company marketed their hard tack as Saloon Pilot crackers, which sounded classier than hard tack. The ship's saloon was the dining room for the captains and officers; the manufacturer claimed that their crackers were good enough to serve in the saloon.

*The Hilo Macaroni Company cracker recipe is still a secret, but this recipe for hard tack comes close to the beloved Saloon Pilot cracker.*

Mix the flour, butter, brown sugar, and salt. Slowly add the milk, and mix well. Knead for 5 minutes, until dough is smooth. Roll out on floured board until it is ½ inch thick. Cut into 3-inch rounds or 3-inch squares. Prick all over with fork. Place on baking pan that has been lightly greased or lined with parchment paper. Bake for 30 minutes in 400°F oven until golden brown.

# 'AHI SPRING ROLLS

MAKES 16 ROLLS

1 pound block 'ahi fillet

16 spring roll or lumpia
   wrappers

Salt and pepper to taste

32 fresh basil leaves

16 sun-dried tomatoes,
   rehydrated in hot water,
   drained and cut in halves

2 cups thinly sliced sweet
   onions (approximately
   2 onions)

1 egg white, beaten, to seal
   the rolls

Canola or peanut oil for deep
   frying

## 'AHI SPRING ROLL SAUCE

2 tablespoons balsamic
   vinegar

2 tablespoons light soy sauce

2 tablespoons Dijon mustard

3 tablespoons honey

1 cup olive oil

½ teaspoon black pepper

## KAIKODO

New York and Tokyo art dealers Mary Ann and Howard Rogers opened Restaurant Kaikodo in 2003 and closed it in 2007. It was a classy place to dine.

Kaikodo's first chef was Michael Fennelly, who came to Hilo via Santa Fe and San Francisco. Chef Mike was an accomplished chef and also an artist. I would guess that a mutual interest in art brought him together with the Rogerses.

*Chef Fennelly won "Best in Show" at Taste of Hilo V with these 'ahi spring rolls.*

**To make the sauce:** Put the vinegar, soy sauce, mustard, and honey in a mixing bowl and whisk until smooth. Slowly whisk in the olive oil, then stir in the pepper.

Slice the 'ahi block into 16 pieces.

**To assemble the spring rolls:** For each 'ahi spring roll, place a wrapper on the work surface so it looks like a diamond. Place one slice of 'ahi on the wrapper, three inches from the bottom. Sprinkle the 'ahi with salt and pepper. Place 2 basil leaves across the center of the 'ahi, top with 2 halves of sun-dried tomatoes and an onion slice. Fold the bottom edge of wrapper over the filling, then roll the spring roll away from you, for 2 turns. Fold in the sides of the wrapper, then continue rolling. Moisten the top point with egg white to seal.

Heat the frying oil to 375°F. Fry the spring rolls until they are golden brown. Set them on a paper towel on a plate and let any excess oil drain off.

Arrange the rolls on a serving plate and serve with a small bowl of the sauce.

*Courtesy of Chef Michael Fennelly, Restaurant Kaikodo*

# BLUEBERRY CREAM CHEESE PIE

**MAKES ONE 9-INCH PIE**

1 (8 ounce) package cream
  cheese, softened

¾ cup powdered sugar

1 teaspoon vanilla extract

1 cup heavy cream

1 (21 ounce) can blueberry pie
  filling, chilled

1 (9-inch) baked pie shell

## PARAMOUNT GRILL

Roy and Pauline Yoshioka opened the Paramount Grill in 1948 on Halai Street in Hilo. They sold a tasty combination plate (musubi, takuan, and teri-yaki meat) for only twenty-five cents. Thanks to their cheap, good food, they were very popular with hungry teens who had a little pocket money.

In 1967 Roy and Pauline sold the Paramount Grill and opened Roy's Gourmet on Kino'ole Street. Roy's Gourmet closed in 1986. Folks still remember their blueberry cream cheese pies, liliko'i chiffon pies, and pumpkin cream chiffon pies.

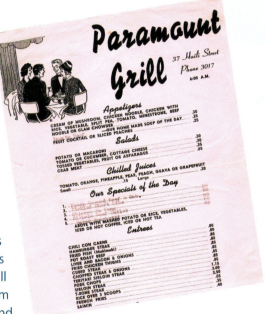

*This blueberry cream cheese pie is as close as I can get to the pies I enjoyed at Paramount Grill and Roy's Gourmet.*

Blend the cream cheese, powdered sugar, and vanilla. Whip the heavy cream and fold it into the cream cheese mixture. Spoon the filling into the baked and cooled pie shell. Top with the blueberry pie filling. Chill several hours before serving.

# CHAPTER 6

# HOMEGROWN: FROM THE LAND

**THE** Big Island is a great place to farm. It has rich volcanic soil and more available agricultural land than any other island. Thanks to the many microclimates found here, farmers can grow an incredible variety of crops. Finally, the Big Island is blessed with skilled and hard-working farmers.

Perhaps the best known Big Island agricultural products are coffee and macadamia nuts. Island farmers also raise cocoa (for chocolate), honey, vanilla, tea, and many tropical vegetables and fruits. We boast the world's biggest cattle ranch, the Parker Ranch, as well as our own goat dairy!

Read on for some fabulous recipes starring our local products.

# LAMB WITH SPICY KIELE O KONA COFFEE SAUCE

SERVES 8

1 (5-7 pound) leg of lamb, boneless

## MARINADE

2 cups brewed 100% Kona coffee

2 tablespoons liliko'i juice

1 tablespoon guava syrup

1 tablespoon green onion, sliced

1 (2-inch) piece fresh ginger, sliced

1 tablespoon balsamic vinegar

3 tablespoons extra virgin olive oil

2 tablespoons Kona coffee syrup

3 cloves garlic, minced

1 tablespoon fennel seeds, roasted and crushed

1 tablespoon soy sauce

Salt and pepper to taste

2 tablespoons olive oil for searing the lamb

## KONA COFFEE

The American missionary Samuel Ruggles brought the first coffee trees to the Big Island in 1828. A sizeable coffee industry developed in the 1880s when immigrant workers finished their indentures on the sugar plantations and started their own coffee farms in Kona.

Many of the new coffee farmers were Japanese immigrants. They bought cheap, three- to five-acre plots in the Kona hill country. By dint of backbreaking work, they turned hilly, rocky land into productive coffee farms. Children helped too: the school season was re-arranged to accommodate the coffee cherry picking season.

The Kona Coffee Cultural Festival is Hawai'i's oldest food festival and the only coffee festival in the United States. It was first held in 1970 when the State Legislature funded a festival to help promote the Kona coffee industry. The festival features a cooking contest in which all entrants must use coffee in some way.

*This recipe won an award in the amateur division of the 2007 Kona Coffee Cook-off.*

**To prepare the lamb:** The lamb should be butterflied—that is, it should be cut and spread open so that it flattens out. The marinade can now penetrate it easily. If you have never butterflied a leg of lamb and are a little daunted by the task, ask the butcher to butterfly it for you.

**To prepare the marinade:** Mix all the ingredients for the marinade in a 1-gallon re-sealable bag. Add the lamb. Put the bag in the refrigerator and let the lamb marinate overnight. Turn it over occasionally to be sure that all the lamb is evenly marinated.

(continued on page 122)

(continued from page 121)

## SAUCE

1 cup brewed Kona coffee
½ cup chicken stock
2 tablespoons liliko'i juice
1 tablespoon soy sauce
1 tablespoon tomato paste
2 cloves garlic, sliced
Salt and pepper to taste
½ cup beef stock
1 cup white wine
1 tablespoon balsamic
    vinegar
2 tablespoons guava syrup
1 tablespoon chopped fresh
    basil
1 (2-inch long) Hawaiian chili
    pepper, scored at ¼-inch
    intervals
2 tablespoons butter, to
    finish

## CORNSTARCH SLURRY

1 tablespoon cold brewed
    Kona coffee
2 teaspoons cornstarch

Preheat the oven to 350°F.

Remove the meat from the marinade. Strain the marinade through a sieve into a saucepot. Warm the marinade over low heat.

While the marinade is heating, sear the lamb. Heat 2 tablespoons of olive oil in a large skillet or sauté pan, over medium-high heat. When the oil is hot, add the lamb and sear on both sides.

Place the lamb in a roasting pan and bake for 30-40 minutes or until the thickest part of the lamb reaches an internal temperature of 150°F. Occasionally baste the lamb with the marinade.

*To prepare the sauce:* While the lamb is cooking, make the sauce. Put all the sauce ingredients except the butter and cornstarch slurry into the pan you used to sear the lamb. Don't wash the pan first, as you want the tasty pan juices.

Cook the sauce over medium-low heat for 10 minutes, reducing the mixture slightly. Strain the sauce through a fine-mesh sieve and return it to the pan. Add the pan juices to the sauce and mix well. Add the butter and the slurry and whisk again; cook over medium-low heat until the sauce thickens. You may need to whisk it a few times to smooth out any lumps that might form.

Remove the cooked lamb from the oven and let it rest for 15 minutes before slicing.

Serve the sliced lamb with Kiele O Kona Coffee Sauce and liliko'i mint jelly.

*Courtesy of Barbara Houssel*

# BIG ISLAND HONEY AND LEMON GLAZED CHICKEN BREAST

## MAKES 4 SERVINGS

4 (6 ounces each) skinless
    chicken breasts
Salt and pepper to taste
2 teaspoons olive oil

### GLAZE

1 cup honey (Volcano Island
    Rare Organic White
    Honey)
6 tablespoons lemon juice
2 tablespoons olive oil
4 tablespoons chopped
    parsley
2 teaspoons chopped garlic

## VOLCANO ISLAND HONEY

In 1974 Richard Spiegel started keeping bees, just for fun. His hobby soon became a business; Volcano Island Honey was started in 1980. Today, his silky, smooth, kiawe white honey is sold all over the United States, as well as in Hong Kong, Tokyo, and Singapore.

*Chef Tsuchiyama is Executive Chef at the Kona Village Resort. He created this simple and tasty chicken dish to showcase the local gourmet honey.*

Put the honey, lemon juice, olive oil, parsley, and garlic in a medium-size bowl and mix well. Set aside.

Preheat your oven to 350°F.

Heat the olive oil in an oven-proof skillet or sauté pan over medium-high heat. Season the chicken breasts with salt and pepper, then sear until nicely browned.

Pour the honey glaze over the chicken. Put the skillet in the oven and bake for approximately 10 minutes, or until the chicken is cooked through. Let the chicken rest in a warm area for 5 minutes, then serve hot.

*Courtesy of Chef Mark Tsuchiyama, Kona Village Resort*

# MACADAMIA CARAMEL SHORTBREAD BARS

## MAKES 36 BARS

2 cups flour

½ cup powdered sugar

¼ teaspoon baking powder

2 sticks butter, slightly
softened

½ teaspoon Hawaiian pure
vanilla extract

### FILLING

1 pound unsalted macadamia
nuts, halves and pieces

1½ cups sugar

½ cup water

¾ cup heavy cream

7 ounces butter

### GLAZE

¾ cup heavy cream

3 ounces butter

¼ cup corn syrup

8 ounces cooking chocolate
(use Original Hawaiian
Dark)

## MACADAMIAS

Macadamia nut trees, which are native to Australia, were introduced to the Big Island in 1881. They were first grown extensively in the 1940s. New trees are still being planted, and the island's macadamia crop just keeps getting bigger and bigger.

Local chefs cook fish or chicken in a crust of chopped macadamia nuts; the fatty nuts complement the low-fat meats. Macadamia nuts are also the stars of many a local sweet: cookies, pies, ice creams, and candies, to name a few. Today the Hilo Coffee Company offers coffees from the island's east side.

*This lavish recipe uses one pound of macadamia nuts. It also uses local chocolate from the Original Hawaiian Chocolate Factory, in Kailua-Kona.*

**To make the shortbread:** Preheat the oven to 350°F. Sift the flour, powdered sugar, and baking powder together in a medium-size bowl. Cut the butter into small pieces and cut into the dry mixture. Add the vanilla and blend well. Pat the dough evenly into the bottom of a 9 x 13-inch pan. Prick the crust with a fork, dotting the whole surface with tiny holes. Bake for 20 minutes or until the edges are browned and the crust appears dry and crisp. Cool.

**To make the filling:** Spread the nuts on a baking sheet and lightly toast in a preheated 350°F oven. Remove the nuts and cool them, but leave the oven turned on.

(continued on page 126)

(continued from page 125)

Put the sugar in a saucepan. Add just enough water to liquefy the sugar. Set over high heat and boil rapidly until the sugar begins to caramelize. Swirl the pan gently to allow the caramel to color evenly and continue to cook until the temperature reaches 246°F and is a nice caramel brown color. Pour all the cream in at once. Pour with one hand, in a small steady stream, and whisk with the other hand. Be careful; the sugar syrup will splatter and boil up. Remove the pan from the heat and swirl the mixture until the boiling subsides and the syrup and cream are evenly blended. Lay the butter in pieces over the surface and let it melt. Stir in the melted butter. Stir in macadamia nuts. Let the filling cool slightly, then spread it over the crust.

Bake for about 17 minutes or until the caramel begins to bubble in the center. Remove and cool completely.

**To make the glaze:** Bring the cream, butter, and corn syrup to a boil in a small, heavy saucepan.

Put the chopped chocolate in a medium-size heat-proof bowl. Pour the hot cream mixture over it. Let the filling set for 5 minutes, then stir gently until the chocolate melts and blends evenly. Stir carefully so you do not create bubbles. Pour the chocolate glaze onto the cooled caramel and tip the pan to spread it evenly. Cool completely.

**To serve:** Cut six rows of bars across and lengthwise, making 36. Any uneaten bars should be stored in the refrigerator.

# SEAFOOD FLAN WITH
## HĀMĀKUA PEPEIAO MUSHROOMS & BIG ISLAND GREEN TEA CONSOMMÉ

MAKES 6 SERVINGS

¼ cup chicken breast, diced

¼ cup raw shrimp or Kona lobster, diced

¼ cup thinly julienned fresh Hāmākua pepeiao mushrooms

¼ cup diced fresh Hāmākua shiitake mushrooms

¼ cup fresh sweet corn kernels

¼ cup finely julienned fresh Hirabara spinach

### FLAN

3 large eggs

2½ cups light chicken stock

½ teaspoon salt

1 tablespoon mirin

1 tablespoon light soy sauce

### GARNISH

1½ cups hot brewed Big Island green tea, strained

The tea plant (*Camelia sinensis*) was first introduced to Hawai'i in 1887, but the fledgling tea plantations proved commercial failures. In 1997 Dr. Francis Zee, a research scientist with the USDA, started growing tea again in test plots on the Big Island. He found that tea grew very well in higher locations, such as Volcano. There are now a few small tea farms on the Big Island, producing an expensive but high-quality brew that appeals to tea connoisseurs. Big Island tea is not yet widely available, but if you are lucky enough to beg or buy some of this primo tea, you may want to try this innovative flan recipe.

*'Ōlelo pa'a Faith Ogawa of Glow Hawai'i and Dining by Faith developed this flan, which uses Big Island produce and is garnished with Big Island green tea. It is an upscale version of the familiar chawanmushi.*

Prepare all the solid ingredients and divide them equally between 6 heat-proof cups, bowls, or ramekins.

Beat the eggs in a bowl. In another bowl, mix the room temperature stock, salt, mirin, and light soy sauce. Pour the stock mixture in a thin stream into the beaten egg. Mix well, but do not beat. The surface of the mixture should be free of bubbles or foam. Strain.

Divide the prepared solid ingredients between 6 cups. Ladle the egg stock mixture into the cups. Cover each cup with plastic wrap and set the cups in a hot steamer. Cover steamer and steam over medium heat for 12-15 minutes. The flan should be slightly firm and not runny. Remove from the steamer and divide tea in each cup. Serve hot. During the summer, it can be served chilled.

*Courtesy of 'Ōlelo pa'a Faith Ogawa.*

# BROWNIE SQUARES

**MAKES 6 DOZEN SMALL, RICH BARS**

**CRUST**

1½ sticks (6 ounces) unsalted butter

1 cup sugar

1 large egg, beaten

½ teaspoon Hawaiian pure vanilla extract

2 cups flour

½ teaspoon baking powder

½ teaspoon salt

## ORIGINAL HAWAIIAN CHOCOLATE FACTORY

The Original Hawaiian Chocolate Factory hand-picks, sun-dries, and roasts the local cocoa beans to produce "nibs." These nibs are ground, refined, liquefied, tempered, and poured into molds. The process is exacting; every step has to be done just so. They must be doing it right, though, because it tastes as good as Swiss chocolate.

*This dessert is great for buffets, as it doesn't crumble like ordinary brownies. It makes a pretty stack on a serving platter, and won't fall apart all over your floors or your guests' laps.*

**To make the crust:** Grease a 13 x 9-inch metal baking pan. Line the pan with foil, leaving a 2-inch overhang on both sides. Grease the foil.

Sift or whisk together all the dry ingredients for the crust in a large bowl. Cut the butter into pats, add it to the flour, and cut the butter into the flour mixture with a pastry cutter, or, if you prefer, your fingers. Add the eggs and the vanilla and mix lightly, just enough to bring the dough together in a ball. Press the dough evenly onto the bottom of the baking pan. It's easiest if you cover the dough with plastic wrap and then pat down the dough, as it is sticky. Put the pan into the refrigerator and chill it until the crust is firm, or at least 20 minutes.

Heat the oven to 375°F. Bake the crust until it is golden brown, or approximately 20 minutes. Remove and cool the crust. Leave the oven on; you will need it again.

## FILLING

1½ sticks (6 ounces) unsalted butter

10½ ounces The Original Hawaiian dark chocolate, chopped

1½ cups packed brown sugar

3 large eggs, beaten

1¼ teaspoons Hawaiian pure vanilla extract

¾ cup flour

¼ cup plus 2 tablespoons Dutch cocoa powder

¾ teaspoon salt

1½ cups chopped macadamia nuts

*To make the filling:* While the crust is cooling, melt the butter, chocolate, and brown sugar in a saucepan over moderate heat, stirring occasionally. The mixture should be shiny and smooth. Remove the chocolate mixture from the heat and cool slightly.

In a separate bowl, whisk the eggs and vanilla together. Add a little of the chocolate mixture to the eggs and mix well. Add a little more, and whisk again. Pour in the rest of the chocolate mixture. Whisk in the flour, cocoa, and salt. Stir in the chopped macadamia nuts.

*To assemble the brownies:* Spread the brownie batter over the cooled crust and put the pan back in the preheated 375°F oven. Bake the brownies until they are set, or about 20 minutes. Remove the pan from the oven and set it on a rack so that air can circulate under the bottom. It should take from 1½ to 2 hours for the brownies to cool completely.

*To serve:* Run a heavy knife under hot water, then wipe it dry. Cut the brownies into 1-inch squares.

# LILIKO'I GRANITA

**MAKES 16
(4 OUNCE) SERVINGS**

3 cups water

1½ cups white wine

1½ cups sugar

¾ cup pure liliko'i juice

¾ cup fresh lemon juice

3 tablespoons pure Hawaiian
   vanilla extract

## HAWAIIAN VANILLA COMPANY

Hawaiian Vanilla Company, located in Pa'auilo, is the first commercial vanilla farm in the United States. The rain, sun, cool breezes, and rich soil of Pa'auilo are ideal for vanilla cultivation. Tracy Reddekopp and her husband, Jim, kindly gave me a few of their vanilla recipes.

*Here is a refreshing palate cleanser to serve between courses of an elegant meal. It's also a perfect pick-me-up on a hot day.*

Combine the water and sugar in a medium-size pot and bring to a boil. Remove from the heat. Chill the mixture in the refrigerator for at least one hour.

Add the white wine to the sugar syrup. Mix the liliko'i juice with the lemon juice and vanilla extract. Combine the wine syrup and the juices, mix well, and pour the granita into a long, shallow container (one that will fit into your freezer). What you need is surface: the more surface area exposed to the cold, the faster the granita will form ice crystals.

Every 30-45 minutes, take a fork and scrape the frozen mixture to stir up the ice crystals. Repeat for 3-4 hours until the granita reaches the desired texture, an icy slush.

About 15-20 minutes before serving, remove the container from freezer and scrape with a fork one last time. Then spoon into glasses (champagne flutes make a dramatic presentation) and garnish with a sprig of fresh thyme or mint.

*Courtesy of the Hawaiian Vanilla Company*

# SPICY HAWAIIAN VANILLA COARSE GROUND MUSTARD

## SPICY HAWAIIAN VANILLA COARSE GROUND MUSTARD

½ cup mustard seeds (yellow, brown, or a combination of both)

2 tablespoons dry mustard

1 tablespoon Hawai'i pure vanilla extract

1 cup apple cider vinegar

¼ cup onion, finely chopped

3 tablespoons light brown sugar

2 garlic cloves, minced

¾ teaspoon salt

¼ teaspoon dried tarragon

¼ teaspoon ground cinnamon

1 Hawaiian vanilla bean

## HAWAIIAN VANILLA-HONEY MUSTARD (MAKES 1 CUP)

¼ cup mayonnaise

5 tablespoons lehua honey

3 tablespoons Dijon mustard

2 tablespoons apple cider vinegar

1 tablespoon Hawai'i pure vanilla extract

Combine the mustard seeds, dry mustard, and vanilla extract. Cover and let sit on the counter overnight.

Combine the vinegar, onion, brown sugar, garlic, salt, tarragon, and cinnamon in a medium-size saucepan. Bring this mixture to a boil over medium-high heat, then reduce the heat slightly and boil, uncovered, until the mixture has been reduced by half; this should take anywhere from 7 to 10 minutes.

Strain the vinegar mixture through a sieve. Discard the residue in the sieve. Pour the liquid into a bowl of a food processor fitted with a blade attachment. Add the mustard seed mixture and process for 2 minutes, or until the seeds are chopped but not puréed. Pour the mustard back into the saucepan and cook it until thick, stirring often.

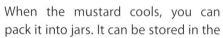

When the mustard cools, you can pack it into jars. It can be stored in the cupboard until opened; once opened, it should be kept in the refrigerator.

## HAWAIIAN VANILLA-HONEY MUSTARD

Mix together and let sit for at least 1 minute before serving. This mustard is great as a salad dressing, pretzel dip, or sandwich spread.

*Courtesy of Hawaiian Vanilla Company*

# WAILEA SPICY HEARTS OF PALM SALAD

**MAKES 4 SERVINGS**

1 (6-inch) piece of heart of palm

2 tablespoons Sriracha hot chili sauce

¼ cup fish sauce or nam pla

⅓ cup brown sugar

⅓ cup freshly squeezed lime juice

3 cloves garlic, pressed

¼ cup chopped cilantro leaves

**GARNISH**

2 tablespoons chopped roasted macadamia nuts

4 Hāmākua Country Springs cocktail tomatoes, quartered

12 (21-25 size) large shrimp, deveined, peeled

## WAILEA AGRICULTURAL GROUP

Hearts of palm is also known as "swamp cabbage." Appealing? NOT! Chefs discovered that hearts of palm were delightful whether sliced, diced, blanched, lightly sautéed, or stir-fried. Hearts of palm is an expensive ingredient, found only in fancy, white-table-cloth restaurants. A good business for entrepreneurs! Wailea Agricultural Group owners Leslie Hill and Michael Crowell started production of hearts of palm in 1997 and now turn out 120 tons a year on 35 acres.

Cut the heart of palm into 2-inch-long julienne strips and set aside.

Mix the hot chili sauce, fish sauce, brown sugar, lime juice, and garlic in a bowl. Add the slivered heart of palm and gently mix. Then add the chopped cilantro leaves; lightly toss the salad to mix it well.

Put the shrimp in a pot of boiling salted water; reduce the heat to low and simmer for 5 minutes. Remove the shrimp from the water and drain.

*To serve:* Divide the salad between four salad plates. Garnish each salad with chopped macadamia nuts, 3 shrimp, and 4 tomato wedges.

# MACADAMIA NUT CRUSTED MAHIMAHI WITH WASABI CREAM SAUCE

## MAKES 4 SERVINGS

1 pound fresh mahimahi
    fillets
2 tablespoons canola oil
¼ cup chopped parsley

### MACADAMIA NUT CRUST
½ cup macadamia nuts
1½ cups panko
Salt and white pepper

### WASABI CREAM SAUCE
2 tablespoons shallots,
    minced
½ cup dry white wine
½ cup fish stock
¾ cup heavy cream
1 tablespoon fresh, grated
    wasabi
1 tablespoon water
2 teaspoons cornstarch + 2
    teaspoons cold water, to
    thicken the sauce

### GARNISH
Flakes of fresh parsley to
    taste

## YAMASHIROS

Lance Yamashiro still works the sixty-acre Volcano farm that his grandfather, Jiro Yamashiro, started in 1942. Today Lance raises several varieties of daikon, head cabbage, Chinese cabbage, broccoli, and leafy red and green lettuce. Lance is best known, however, for his wasabi.

Wasabi is hard to grow, and consequently is very expensive. (Most of the wasabi paste we eat isn't real wasabi, but horseradish.) In the wild, wasabi grows on the edge of running streams. Lance experimented with raising wasabi grown in dirt, without running water. He planted a half-acre of wasabi under shade cloth, coaxing it to grow. Now he produces fresh, Island-grown wasabi commercially. Wasabi farmers from Japan come to marvel at his enterprise!

*Chef Colin Nakagawa of Seaside Restaurant shared this tasty fish dish, which uses fresh wasabi.*

**How to prepare fresh wasabi:** Peel the rhizome (root) with a potato peeler, then dip in cold spring or bottled water. Grate the peeled root with a ginger grater. Continue dipping in water and grating until you have enough wasabi for immediate use.

Spray the leftover wasabi with water, wrap it in a paper towel, and store it in the refrigerator. It should stay fresh for 2-3 weeks. It is such a treat that you will not find it difficult to use the whole root in that time.

***To prepare the crust:*** Combine the nuts, panko, salt, and pepper in a food processor. Blend until mixture is finely ground.

***To prepare the sauce:*** Put the wine and shallots in a large saucepan and cook over medium heat until most of the wine has evaporated. Add the fish stock, heavy cream, and wasabi. Bring the sauce to a boil, then lower the heat to medium-low. Add the cornstarch slurry and stir. The sauce should thicken nicely; whisk to combine and remove any lumps.

***To prepare the fish:*** Coat the fish fillets with the macadamia nut crust mixture. Heat the canola oil in a large sauté pan or skillet; sauté the fillets until they are golden brown.

***To serve:*** Pour ¼ cup of wasabi cream sauce in the center of each of 4 serving plates. Place the cooked fish on the sauce. Garnish with parsley flakes.

*Courtesy of Chef Colin Nakagawa, Seaside Restaurant*

# CHERRY TOMATO COMPOTE

**MAKES 8 SERVINGS**

1 basket red and gold cherry
   tomatoes (approximately
   1 pound)

1½ cups large tomatoes,
   diced and puréed in
   blender

¼ cup + 2 tablespoons +
   ½ cup sugar

1 cup water

½ medium-size lemon, sliced
   thin and chopped (include
   the peel)

1 cup sultana raisins

## HĀMĀKUA COUNTRY SPRING FARMS

When you think of Hāmākua Country Spring Farms, you think of tomatoes. But Richard Ha, the owner, grows more than tomatoes; he also grows cucumbers, peppers, beets, radishes, green onions, lettuce, watercress, and bananas. Local chefs count on him for high-quality produce; in fact, they tell him what to grow. He started growing hydroponic lettuce at the suggestion of Chef Alan Wong.

*Here's a recipe that uses his signature tomatoes.*

*Lakeisha Germany-Ross was an eleventh grader at Connections Charter School when she won the grand prize in the second annual "You Say Tomato" recipe contest, sponsored by Hāmākua Country Spring Farms. Lakeisha made a sweet tomato compote and served it over a rich Italian pudding, or budino.*

Preheat the oven to 325°F.

Cut the cherry tomatoes into sixths and place seed side up on a mesh rack. Sprinkle ¼ cup sugar over the tomatoes. Put the tomato-covered rack on a cookie sheet, to catch any drips, then put it in the oven. Bake it for 15 minutes; then pull it out and sprinkle 2 more tablespoons of sugar on the tomatoes. Put it back in the oven and bake until the tomatoes are dry but not brittle. This should take about 1 to 1½ hours.

When the tomatoes are almost dry, start on the next steps. Put the ½ sugar and 1 cup water in a medium saucepan; bring to a boil. Add the chopped lemon. Simmer the lemon syrup for 10 minutes.

The roasted tomatoes should be finished by now. Add the roasted tomatoes and the raisins to the mixture. Cook until the mixture is bubbling fiercely.

Add the tomato purée and cook for 4 more minutes. Stir with a heatproof spatula so that the compote does not scorch on the bottom of the pan. Remove the compote from the heat and let it cool to room temperature.

5 ounces softened cream
cheese

13 ounces mascarpone
cheese

3 large eggs

⅓ cup plus 1 tablespoon
sugar

1¾ tablespoons freshly
squeezed lemon juice

Finely grated zest of ½
orange

Finely grated zest of ½ lemon

# BUDINO

Preheat the oven to 325°F. Spray 8 ramekins with oil and line the bottoms with circles of parchment paper. Put them in a large, heavy pan (a roasting pan works well). You will later fill this pan with water so that the budino is baking in a water bath.

Using an electric mixer if possible, beat the cream cheese until smooth. Add the sugar gradually and beat until completely blended. Add the mascarpone and beat until smooth. Add the eggs, one at a time, beating well after each addition. Be sure to scrape the sides of the bowl. Add the orange and lemon zests and mix.

Pour the budino into the prepared ramekins in the large pan. Pull out an oven rack, put the large pan on the rack, and fill the pan with boiling-hot water. The water should come up to the middle of the ramekins. Slide the rack carefully back into the oven. You might want to wear oven mitts for this step. The boiling water may splash.

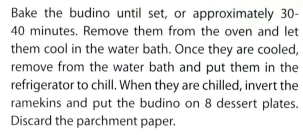

Bake the budino until set, or approximately 30-40 minutes. Remove them from the oven and let them cool in the water bath. Once they are cooled, remove from the water bath and put them in the refrigerator to chill. When they are chilled, invert the ramekins and put the budino on 8 dessert plates. Discard the parchment paper.

**To serve:** Top the plates of budino with the tomato compote.

*Courtesy of Lakeisha Germany-Ross*

# SEARED HIRABARA BABY ROMAINE GREENS WITH ROAST BIG ISLAND TENDERLOIN OF BEEF

Pam and Kurt Hirabara grow eight varieties of baby lettuce on their Kamuela farm. Lettuce is a cold weather crop and loves Kamuela's cool climate. Their baby romaine is outstanding!

**To prepare the glaze:** Combine all ingredients and store in a container until ready to use.

**To prepare the pesto:** Bring a saucepan of water to a boil; add some salt to the water. Blanch the arugula in the boiling water, stirring so that the leaves blanch evenly. Blanch for about 15 seconds. Drain the leaves, then plunge them into an ice water bath so that they cool quickly and do not continue cooking. Drain, use your hands to squeeze all the water out of the arugula, and drain again.

Put the arugula, olive oil, pine nuts, garlic, salt, and pepper in a blender. Add the cheese and pulse briefly. Transfer to a bowl and adjust the seasoning.

### MAKES 6 SERVINGS

2 pounds roast tenderloin of beef, sliced thin

12 baby romaine leaves, cut in half lengthwise

2 medium-size tomatoes, cut in wedges

1 medium-size sweet onion, sliced thin

4 ounces Hāmākua kea-shimeji mushrooms

Red wine vinegar

Olive oil

## GLAZE FOR SEARED ROMAINE LETTUCE

¼ cup soy sauce

1 tablespoon dry sherry wine

1 tablespoon oyster sauce

1 tablespoon red wine vinegar

½ teaspoon thick soy sauce

1½ teaspoons chili garlic sauce

1 clove garlic, minced

1 teaspoon ginger, minced

## ARUGULA PESTO SAUCE

2⅓ cups firmly packed fresh arugula

⅔ cup olive oil

3 tablespoons pine nuts

1 clove garlic

Salt and pepper to taste

¼ cup freshly grated Parmesan cheese

## GARNISH

Thinly sliced Parmesan cheese

Fresh ground black pepper

**To sear the romaine lettuce leaves:** Heat a large frying pan on high heat. Add just enough olive oil to coat the pan lightly. Sear the romaine lettuce, turn over. Add half the onions and all the mushrooms. Drizzle glaze over the romaine, onions, and mushrooms, then shake the frying pan back and forth so that the glaze will be evenly distributed. Turn the greens, onions, and mushrooms once again and repeat the process.

**Note:** The glaze is very concentrated, so use it sparingly. It is likely that you will not use all the glaze you prepare. The entire process is quick and can be done in 2 minutes or less.

**To assemble the salad:** Transfer the seared greens to a platter. Arrange the roast tenderloin of beef over the greens. Garnish with the tomatoes and onion slices. Drizzle some red wine vinegar and olive oil. Add a dollop of arugula pesto sauce, then arrange the Parmesan cheese on top. Finish with freshly ground black pepper. Serve immediately.

*Courtesy of ʻŌlelo paʻa Faith Ogawa*

# SMOOTHIE

**MAKES 1 SERVING**

One whole banana, peeled
    and frozen
One cup frozen, peeled,
    cubed papaya
5 frozen strawberries, green
    stems removed
Juice from ½ orange
¼ cup fresh apple juice

## WHAT'S SHAKIN

Patsy and Tim Withers tend twenty acres of fruit trees in Pepe'ekeo. They serve many of these fruits in their delightful restaurant, What's Shakin, which is famous for its smoothies. Patsy and Tim don't need to add sugar or ice to their smoothies; the natural sweetness of the fresh-picked fruit is all that is needed.

*Note that the quantities aren't exact. Bananas vary in size, as do strawberries and oranges. If the fruit you are using is exceptionally large or small, you may need to adjust the recipe.*

Blend all ingredients until smooth. You may add yogurt, protein powder, or spirulina before blending.

*Courtesy of What's Shakin*

# GOAT CHEESE WON TONS

**MAKES 25-30 WONTONS**

1 (12 ounce) package round man doo wrappers
1 (6 ounce) package Hawai'i Island Goat Dairy's smoked goat cheese
½ cup diced prosciutto (¼-inch dice)
¼ cup chopped macadamia nuts
1 egg white
Canola oil for deep frying

**PINEAPPLE MARMALADE**
**MAKES 2 CUPS**

2 cups chopped fresh pineapple (you can substitute canned crushed pineapple)
1 cup sugar
Pinch of crushed chili flakes

### HAWAI'I ISLAND GOAT DAIRY: GOAT CHEESE

Dick and Heather Threlfall, of Hawai'i Island Goat Dairy, have been making plain and feta chèvre, or goat cheese, since 2001. They graze their 110 dairy goats on 10 acres of macadamia nut orchard. I can testify that their happy goats make great cheese.

*These fried wontons make a great pūpū. Serve them with Sam Choy's pineapple marmalade; that recipe follows.*

Separate the egg; save the yolk to thicken a sauce or a custard.

Mix the smoked goat cheese with the diced prosciutto.

Brush the edges of a man doo wrapper with egg white. Place a teaspoonful of the cheese mixture in the center of the man doo wrapper. Sprinkle the cheese with ½ teaspoon of chopped nuts. Fold the man doo wrapper in half, forming a half-circle won ton. Lightly press down on the edges to seal the won ton. Heat oil for frying to 350°F in a deep, heavy pot or a wok. Deep-fry the half moons until they are golden brown, or about 2-3 minutes on each side. Drain them on paper towels. Serve the won tons warm, with pineapple marmalade on the side.

## PINEAPPLE MARMALADE

Put the pineapple and sugar in a heavy saucepan and cook over medium heat. Bring the mixture to a boil, then simmer uncovered until the marmalade thickens to a syrupy consistency, stirring occasionally. This should take about 45 minutes for fresh pineapple, or 30 minutes if you are using canned crushed pineapple. Remove the marmalade from the heat and let it cool. Put into jars and refrigerate.

*Courtesy of Chef Sam Choy*

# ALI'I OYSTER MUSHROOM RISOTTO

## MAKES 4–6 SERVINGS

2 tablespoons olive oil

2 tablespoons minced shallot

1 cup Arborio rice

4 ounces finely diced Ali`i oyster mushrooms

3 ounces dry white wine

3½ to 4 cups hot chicken stock

¼ cup grated Parmesan cheese

1 ounce dried porcini mushrooms (optional)

## HAMAKUA HERITAGE MUSHROOMS

Hamakua Heritage Mushrooms is located in a state-of-the-art, environmentally controlled 16,000 square foot production facility in Laupahoehoe.

Robert and Janice Stanga have shimeji, gray oyster, alii oyster, and nameko mushrooms and are working on pepeiao or wood-ear, Italian pioppini or black poplar mushrooms.

*Risotto can be bland if not sparked with some contrasting flavors and textures. Here, the firm texture of the Ali'i oyster mushrooms complements the creamy risotto. If you decide to add the optional porcini mushrooms, they will bring a rich, dark flavor to the dish.*

If using dried porcini, soak them in ¼ cup of hot stock for 20 minutes. Drain and chop the mushrooms. Save the soaking liquid.

Heat the oil in a large sauté pan or skillet over medium heat. Add the minced shallot and sauté for a few minutes. Add the rice and mushrooms and cook, stirring, for a minute or so. Do not brown the shallots or rice. Add the wine, followed by the stock, ½ cup at a time. Stir frequently and add stock as needed.

As the risotto becomes creamy, test a grain of rice now and then. Stop adding stock when the texture is smooth with just a hint of al dente firmness at the core of the rice. Stir in the grated Parmesan cheese. If you want to add the optional porcini mushrooms, add them now, together with their soaking liquid.

Serve as a side dish.

*Courtesy of Hāmākua Heritage Mushrooms*

# FROM THE SEA

**HAWAIIANS,** and Hawai'i residents, have always eaten lots of wild-caught fish. The Big Island is famous for its fishing grounds. But as Hawai'i's population has expanded, and development and overfishing have degraded many of our fisheries, Islanders have increasingly turned to aquaculture.

Some of the aquaculture is small-scale. Freshwater tilapia and catfish are easy to raise and many aquaculture enthusiasts have tanks in their backyards.

Other ventures are much larger and more capital-intensive. They can be found at the Natural Energy Laboratory of Hawai'i Authority (NELHA) science and technology park in Kailua-Kona, at Keahole Point. The park rents space to educational, scientific, and commercial tenants. Those commercial tenants include several aquaculture firms.

NELHA pumps up cold, deep seawater from offshore. This seawater is rich in nutrients, pathogen-free, and ideal for aquaculture. Tenants install tanks and raise various fish, shellfish, and seaweed in the cold, clean water.

# ASIAN-STYLE STEAMED KONA KAMPACHI

MAKES 2 SERVINGS

2–6 ounces kampachi fillet

Salt and pepper to taste

4–6 ti leaves or 1 banana leaf

2 cups cooked jasmine rice

2 tablespoons roughly
   chopped ginger

1 stalk lemongrass, smashed

¼ cup soy sauce

1 tablespoon peanut oil

Furikake to taste

## KONA BLUE

The story of Kona Blue starts in 2001 when marine biologists Dale Sarver and Neil Anthony Sims committed to raising high-quality, sushi-grade fish at Keahole. It took three years of research and several rounds of investment, but by 2004 Kona Blue had started the first integrated hatchery and offshore fish farm in the United States.

One of Kona Blue's most popular products is kampachi, or Hawaiian yellowtail. Thanks to the NELHA park's location, next to the Kailua-Kona International Airport, the kampachi can easily be shipped worldwide.

*The good folks at Kona Blue gave me the following recipe, which highlights the clean taste of the farmed fish.*

Season the kampachi fillet with salt and pepper.

Place the ti leaves side-by-side, slightly overlapping, so that they form a wrapper wide enough to enclose the fish. Spread the cooked rice in the center of the wrapper. Place the fish on top of the rice, then top the fish with ginger, lemongrass, soy sauce, and peanut oil. Sprinkle with furikake.

Fold the sides and ends of the ti leaves over the fish so that the package is completely sealed. You may want to tie the packet shut with cooking twine. Place in a steamer over boiling water for 12 minutes.

*Courtesy of Kona Blue*

# KONA KAMPACHI CARPACCIO WITH ĀNUENUE HŌʻIʻO OGO RELISH & GINGER PONZU SAUCE

### MAKES 8-10 SERVINGS

2 pounds fresh filLet of Kona kampachi, sliced thin

### ANUENUE HŌʻIʻO OGO RELISH

3 cups fresh hōʻiʻo fern shoots (warabi), blanched and cooled (approximately 1 bunch)

1 cup diced sweet onion (approximately ½ onion)

1 cup diced Japanese cucumber (approximately 1 cucumber)

½ cup diced red bell pepper (approximately ½ pepper)

½ cup diced yellow bell pepper (approximately ½ pepper)

¼ cup pickled ginger

1 cup diced tomato (approximately 1 tomato)

½ cup chopped ogo seaweed

### GINGER PONZU SAUCE

⅔ cup soy sauce

⅓ cup mirin

⅓ cup fresh lemon juice

1 tablespoon sugar

1 tablespoon minced ginger

Fresh Hawaiian chili pepper to taste

### GARNISH

Shichimi togarashi, (Japanese red pepper mix)

10 fresh chiso leaves, thinly sliced

Fresh red radish, thinly sliced

*Here's another, fancier kampachi recipe.*

*Carpaccio is just another name for thinly sliced raw meat or fish. It's not safe to eat wild-caught kampachi as carpaccio or sushi, because the fish is often infested with parasites. Cultivated kampachi, however, is parasite-free and safe to eat.*

*ThIS dish is garnished with shichimi togarashi, a complex Japanese seasoning that is made with mandarin orange, sesame seeds, poppy seeds, hemp seeds, nori, and sansho. Sansho is, botanically, Zanthoxylum sancho, a hot spice in the family of Sichuan peppers.*

**To make the relish:** Mix ferns, onion, cucumber, peppers, tomato, and ogo in a bowl.

**To make the sauce:** Mix all ingredients in a bowl.

**To serve:** Arrange the kampachi carpaccio in a circle on a serving platter. Sprinkle with shichimi togarashi, chiso leaves, and sliced radish. Arrange ogo relish in the center of the platter. Drizzle with the ponzu sauce. Serve immediately.

(All diced vegetables should be cut into approximately ¼-inch dice.)

*Courtesy of ʻŌlelo paʻa Faith Ogawa*

# ABALONE: STEAKS, FRIED, SUSHI, SASHIMI

## BIG ISLAND ABALONE

Big Island Abalone has been operating a ten-acre aquaculture farm since 1997. It is the largest abalone farm in the world and sells to high-end restaurants in Hawai'i and Tokyo, Japan. "Iron Chef" Morimoto uses Big Island abalone in his restaurants.

*The following recipes for abalone may seem too simple, but abalone has such wonderful taste that it can stand by itself as steaks, sushi, or sashimi.*

## PREPARING FRESH ABALONE

If you're starting with fresh abalone rather than prepared abalone meat, you'll need to prepare the abalone. Here's how.

If you can't process the abalone right away, you can store the fresh abalone meat-side down in a bucket of seawater, stored in a cool place. Abalone can live up to three days this way. When you're ready to shuck the abalone, you may want to cover your counter or table with newspaper or plastic. Abalone is messy.

Open the shell with a heavy knife. Start at the shallow side and work your way around the shell. You must start at the shallow end; otherwise you run the risk of puncturing the guts of the abalone and contaminating the meat.

Use an extremely sharp knife to cut off the guts. Insert the point and move the knife in a circle. The guts are connected to the abalone meat by a small layer of tissue; you want to cut AROUND this tissue. Be very careful not to puncture the guts. Remove the black "lips" and the tough part of the "foot."

Discard the guts and lips immediately. Don't let them touch the meat.

(continued on page 148)

(continued from page 147)

Abalone meat can be kept on ice until you are ready to use it, or frozen for up to two months.

## ABALONE STEAKS

*If the abalone is tender enough, you won't need to slice and pound it. You can cook it whole, as an abalone steak. Make sure to save and clean the shells when you process the abalone so that you can serve them in the shell.*

**To prepare the abalone steaks:** Score the upper side of the body with ½-inch deep diagonal slices, 1 inch apart. Heat the olive oil, butter, and garlic in a sauté pan. When the garlic is lightly seared, put the abalone in the pan, meat side down, and cook until the surface of the meat is lightly seared. Don't overcook! Pour the soy sauce into the pan and lightly coat the abalone steaks.

**To serve:** Place abalone in the shell and garnish with sliced lemon.

## FRIED ABALONE

To make the seasoned flour, mix 1 cup flour, 1 teaspoon black pepper, and 2 teaspoons salt. You may have to double or triple the recipe if you are making a lot of abalone.

Cut the abalone into ¼-inch slices against the grain of the meat. You may need to pound the meat until it is tender. You can do this with a meat tenderizing mallet. Stop at intervals to feel the meat; you don't want to pound too much. Stop when the meat feels soft. Dip the pounded slices in seasoned flour, then shake off the excess flour. Heat the oil in a sauté pan over high heat. Sauté the abalone for 30 seconds on each side. Don't overcook! Overcooking will toughen the abalone.

## ABALONE SUSHI AND SASHIMI

You won't even need to cook abalone if you've carefully cleaned, sliced, and tenderized it. Just cut into thin, serving-size slices and enjoy.

### ABALONE STEAKS
### SERVES 4

4 fresh abalone
1 tablespoon olive oil
2 tablespoons butter
1 tablespoon sliced fresh
   garlic
2 tablespoons soy sauce
Lemon slices for garnish

### FRIED ABALONE

Abalone
Seasoned flour
Vegetable oil

# STEAMED MOI WITH LUP CHEONG, GREEN ONIONS, AND GINGER

**MAKES 4 SERVINGS**

1 (1½ pound) fresh moi or Pacific threadfin, scaled, cleaned

½ teaspoon salt

1 garlic clove, minced

½ cup julienned Hilo ginger

1 Chinese lup cheong sweet sausage, sliced

2–3 tablespoons peanut oil

2 stalks green onions, finely julienned

5 sprigs Chinese cilantro

2 tablespoons soy sauce

## UWAJIMA FISHERIES

Uwajima Fisheries, in Keahole, raises flounder, tilapia, moi, and kampachi; it also grows ogo, the delectable red seaweed.

Local cooks are particularly happy to be able to buy moi. Moi is a tasty, but rare, fish. In the past, one rarely saw moi in the market. Only fishermen and their friends ate moi with any frequency. Now that it is farm-raised, we can all enjoy moi.

*This recipe from Sam Choy's father is easy and tasty. The addition of lup cheong gives this dish another dimension of flavor.*

Put the moi on a heatproof dish and sprinkle it with salt, minced garlic, and a little of the julienned ginger. Stuff the fish with the lup cheong sausage, reserving a few sausage slices. Arrange these slices on top of the fish. Steam the fish in a steamer basket for 8–10 minutes.

Heat peanut oil in a small saucepan until it starts to smoke. Sprinkle the green onions, the remaining ginger, and the cilantro over the steamed fish. Pour hot oil over fish; it should sizzle. Drizzle with soy sauce and serve.

*Courtesy of Chef Sam Choy*

# TAKO POKE (OCTOPUS POKE)

**MAKES 4 SERVINGS**

½ pound tako, cut into bite-
   sized pieces
1 cup diced firm, ripe
   tomato (½-inch dice)
   (approximately 1 tomato)
½ cup minced sweet onion
   (approximately half a
   medium-size onion)
2 ounces brown ogo, finely
   chopped
Salt to taste
Sesame oil to taste
Chili pepper to taste

## ROYAL HAWAIIAN SEA FARMS

Royal Hawaiian Sea Farms, located in NELHA's Keahole technology park, raises ogo. They grow five varieties: long brown, long green, long red, thick green, and thick brown. They sell to local chefs and restaurants on the U.S. West Coast where ogo has been over-harvested and is rare.

*Ogo enhances this poke with its sweet crunch.*

Combine all the ingredients in a serving bowl and serve as a pūpū.

# KONA COLD LOBSTER

## KONA COLD LOBSTER

Brothers Joe and Phil Wilson, who raised lobsters for ten years in Southern California, started Kona Cold Lobster in 1986. They knew all the tricks of the trade and were soon producing fine, fresh lobsters.

Joe was willing to tell me the secret to cooking lobster. "When they are red, they are dead and cooked." As soon as they change color, they should be removed from the water. Even after they have been removed from the water, the shell retains the heat and the lobster meat keeps cooking—for as long as 10 minutes. Joe believes that 99% of the lobster he sells ends up overcooked. Because lobster meat has next to no fat (less than turkey breast!), overcooked meat dries out and toughens.

Award-winning chef Alan Wong would never overcook his lobsters. He has been buying Kona Cold lobsters ever since he served as Executive Chef for the Canoe House restaurant at the Mauna Lani Resort in Waikoloa.

*Alan gave me this simple recipe.*

Dunk a live lobster, head first, in boiling water. When the shell turns red, remove the lobster from the water. Crack the shell open and dip the meat in hot, melted butter. Enjoy!

*Courtesy of Chef Alan Wong*

# KONA COLD LOBSTER AU GRATIN

### MAKES 6 SERVINGS

6 Kona Cold lobsters, boiled
   in shell
2 cups fine bread crumbs
½ cup melted butter

### LOBSTER SAUCE

1½ cups mayonnaise
½ cup parsley, finely
   chopped
4 tablespoons fresh lemon
   juice
1 tablespoon Worcestershire
   sauce
Hot pepper sauce to taste
Salt and pepper to taste
1½ tablespoons Dijon
   mustard
⅓ cup sherry

Split the cooked lobsters lengthwise. Remove the whole meat from the lobster tails and arrange the meat in six shallow buttered baking dishes, one for each serving.

Preheat your oven to 350°F.

Blend the mayonnaise, parsley, lemon juice, Worcestershire sauce, hot pepper sauce, salt, pepper, mustard, and sherry in a bowl. Pour this sauce over each dish of lobster.

Sprinkle bread crumbs over each lobster dish and drizzle with melted butter. Bake the lobster dishes at 350°F for 30 minutes, until the sauce is bubbling and the crumbs are lightly toasted.

# SWEET AND SOUR TILAPIA WITH ISLAND FRUITS

**MAKES 4 SERVINGS**

4 large tilapia, scaled and cleaned
½ cup cornstarch
Oil for deep frying

**SWEET AND SOUR SAUCE**

½ cup sugar
1 cup vinegar
2 cups pineapple juice
2 tablespoons ketchup
1 Hawaiian chili pepper
1 tablespoon cornstarch
½ cup cold water
1 tablespoon butter
½ cup pineapple chunks
½ cup sliced starfruit
½ cup Ka'ū orange, sectioned
½ cup diced half-ripe but firm papaya
½ cup lychee, whole
½ cup diced honeydew melon
½ cup finely cubed red and yellow
    sweet bell peppers
½ cup cubed, half-ripe, mango bell
    peppers

**GARNISH**

½ cup sliced green onions
    (approximately 1 bunch)
½ cup Chinese parsley leaves
    (approximately 1 bunch parsley)

## OKAMURA FISH FARM

Wayne Okamura started the Okamura Fish Farm in 1996 on 16.3 acres of former cane land in Hāwī, Kohala. Irrigation ditches that once fed cane now supply the water needed for his farm. Wayne raises tilapia, Chinese catfish, and grass carp.

Wayne's favorite product is his tilapia, which he breeds to improve yield and flavor. He is happy to supply the rising demand for tilapia, which chefs appreciate for its reliability and mild flavor. Many chefs are now serving tilapia as a whole fish, arranged beautifully on the finished plate.

*Here is one of Chef Sam Choy's great recipes for tilapia. Sam Choy notes that if the fresh fruits are not available, round onions, tomato wedges, pineapple chunks, and celery slices can be substituted.*

**To make the sweet and sour sauce:** Bring the sugar, vinegar and pineapple juice to a boil in a saucepot over medium heat. Reduce heat to medium. Dissolve the 1 tablespoon of cornstarch in the cold water. Mix the cornstarch slurry into the sauce. Add the ketchup and Hawaiian chili pepper to the simmering sauce.

Diced fruit should be cut into ¼-inch dice. Sauté the bell peppers and all the fruit in the butter, then add the vegetables and fruit to the sweet and sour sauce. Take the sauce off the direct heat, but cover it to keep it warm.

**To fry the tilapia:** Dust the tilapia with cornstarch and deep fry in oil until it is golden brown.

**To serve:** Pour the sauce over cooked fish and garnish with Chinese parsley and green onion.

*Courtesy of Chef Sam Choy*

# FARMERS' MARKETS

**THE** Big Island boasts many farmers' markets.

The Hilo Farmers' Market is located at the corner of Kamehameha Avenue and Mamo Street, in the heart of downtown Hilo. It is officially open on Wednesdays and Saturdays but there are vendors there daily.

The Kino'ole Farmers' Market is held on Saturday from 8:00 a.m. to noon at 1990 Kino'ole Street.

Makulu Farmers' Market is located on highway 130, going towards Pāhoa town. It's open on Sunday from 8:00 a.m. to 2:00 p.m.

Kea'au's Farmers' Market is held in a permanent structure and is open daily.

In Kona, the Keauhou Farmers' Market is held on Saturday at the Keauhou Shopping Center from 8:00 to 11:00 a.m.

Waikoloa Village Farmers' Market is held on Saturday at the Waikoloa Community Church from 7:30 a.m. to 1:00 p.m.

The Waimea Hawaiian Homestead Farmers' Market is open every Saturday from 7:00 a.m. to noon. The first Saturday of the month is bigger, with more vendors and more activity. It is held on the front lawn of the Hawaiian Homes building.

North Kohala holds a farmers' market on Saturdays under the banyan tree across from the Hāwī Post Office. The market is open from 7:00 a.m. to noon.

Pāhoa Farmers' Market is held on Sunday in the Akebono Theatre parking lot from 8:00 a.m. to 3:00 p.m.

Volcano Farmers' Market is held at the Cooper Center, on Wright Road. It is open every Sunday from 6:30 to 9:00 a.m.

Here are some recipes that use produce from the farmers' markets.

# WARABI MIXED RICE

**MAKES 6 SERVINGS**

20 stalks warabi or fern shoots

5 dried shiitake mushrooms, soaked in water

1 (6 ounce) block kamaboko, slivered

2 pieces aburage or fried bean curd, chopped

1 (2-inch square) piece of yam cake or konnyaku, finely sliced

1 (6½ ounce) can minced clams, drained

5 dried shrimps, chopped

1 cup peeled and minced carrot (approximately 1 small carrot)

1 tablespoon canola oil

¼ cup soy sauce

1 heaping tablespoon brown sugar

Salt to taste

6 cups hot cooked rice

*Warabi, also known as hōʻiʻo or bracken fern, grows wild on the east side of the island. You will often find beds of warabi next to a river or stream, as it grows well in moist soil. If you don't want to pick your own, you can buy warabi at a farmers' market or supermarket.*

Wash, clean, and finely chop the warabi. Remove the stems from the shiitake mushrooms, then cut the caps into ¼-inch cubes. Line up your prepared ingredients on the counter, in preparation for stir-frying them.

Heat the canola oil in a large skillet over medium heat. Sauté the warabi, mushrooms, kamaboko, aburage, konnyaku, clams, shrimp, and minced carrot. Combine the soy sauce, sugar, and salt, then stir the mixture into the stir-fried vegetables. Simmer the dish for 5 minutes. Add the rice and mix well.

# CRUNCHY SALMON SALAD

**MAKES 6 SERVINGS**

1 (12 ounce) package (ready cubed) salted salmon (lomi), rinsed and drained

½ pound (approximately 1 bunch) pipinola shoots

½ pound string beans, cut at a slant, each piece 1¼ inches long

1 young pipinola (chayote) fruit, approximately 5 inches long

1½ cups diced Roma tomatoes (½-inch dice)(approximately 5 large tomatoes)

1 cup diced sweet onion (½-inch dice) (approximately 1 onion)

**SAUCE**

1 tablespoon fish sauce or patis

1 tablespoon sweet chili sauce

1 tablespoon water

2 tablespoons brown sugar

1 teaspoon sesame oil

*Pipinola shoots should perhaps be called chayote shoots, as they are the shoots harvested from the plant more commonly known as chayote or mirliton. You can usually buy them at farmers' markets in Hilo.*

*This recipe for pipinola shoots was created by Leonora Takayama, of Hilo. It won first place in the salad division at the first annual Tomato Recipe Contest, sponsored by Hāmākua Country Spring Farms.*

**To prepare the sauce:** Mix together and set aside.

**To prepare the pipinola shoots:** Use only the tender parts of the shoots. Cut them into ¼-inch slices.

**To prepare the pipinola (chayote) fruit:** Trim off the top and bottom of the fruit. Peel. Cut the fruit into quarters, lengthwise, and trim out the seed in the middle. Cut across the quarters to make ¼-inch slices. Soak them in cold water to rinse off the sticky sap.

**To prepare the salad:** In a large pot, bring water to a rolling boil. Parboil the pipinola shoots, string beans, and pipinola. Parboil each kind of vegetable separately, as they all require different cooking times. Pipinola shoots: 1 minute; string beans: 2 minutes; pipinola: 3 minutes.

When the vegetables are just tender, put them in cold water to prevent them from cooking any further. The retained heat in the vegetables might otherwise make them mushy.

Mix all the ingredients in a large bowl. Marinate the salad for a minimum of 1 hour; overnight might be better. Serve when chilled.

*Courtesy of Leonora Takayama*

# CHICKEN TINOLA

**MAKES 6 SERVINGS**

3 pounds skinless, boneless
chicken breasts or thighs

1 (8-inch long) green papaya,
peeled and cut into
wedges

4 garlic cloves, crushed

2 tablespoons julienned fresh
ginger

2 tablespoons canola oil for
sautéing

1 cup sliced onion
(approximately 1 onion)

2 tablespoons patis or fish
sauce

4 cups water

½ cup young marungay
leaves

*Marungay leaves are harvested from the moringa oleifera tree, or marungay tree, which is native to the Philippines. They impart a citrus-like and slightly bitter taste to food. You can usually buy these leaves at Hilo's Farmers' Market. Here's a chicken dish that uses marungay leaves.*

Rinse the chicken and cut it into bite-size pieces.

Heat the oil in a large pot or Dutch oven. Add the ginger and garlic and sauté ginger until fragrant. Add the sliced onions and cook until the onions are translucent. Add the chicken pieces and cook for approximately 10 minutes. Add the patis and 4 cups water. Cover and simmer for 30 minutes. Add papaya wedges, cover and simmer for 15 minutes. Add the marungay leaves and allow the stew to boil for 3 minutes.

# PICKLED YOUNG GINGER

**MAKES 1/2 GALLON OF PICKLES**

½ gallon peeled and
   sliced young ginger
   (approximately 2 pounds)
3 tablespoons coarse salt
3 cups sugar
1½ cups rice vinegar
¾ cup water
1 teaspoon red food coloring

*Once a year young ginger from the farms on the Hāmākua Coast is sold at the farmers' markets in Hilo. This white and tender ginger is perfect for making pickled ginger, a delectable homemade garnish for sushi.*

Scrape the skin off the young ginger and slice it into paper thin slices. A cook's mandoline might be useful here. Put the ginger in a container with a lid; add salt to the ginger slices and mix well. Cover the container and let stand overnight.

The next day, put the ginger in a colander and drain, then squeeze out the rest of the water with your hands. Do not rinse the ginger! Mix the sugar, vinegar, water, and food coloring in a saucepot and bring the marinade to a rolling boil over medium-high heat. Put the ginger in the sterilized jars, then pour the hot pickling mixture over ginger. Let the ginger stand at room temperature until it has cooled.

Serve the pickled ginger with sushi. Any unused ginger should be refrigerated. It will last in the refrigerator for several months.

# PUNA PAPAYA CRÈME BRÛLÉE

**MAKES 24 SERVINGS**

1 vanilla bean

4 cups heavy cream

¼ teaspoon salt

⅔ cup sugar

1 cup ripe papaya purée
(usually takes 2–3
medium-size papayas)

Zest of 1 medium-
size lemon, finely
chopped

8 large egg yolks

2 tablespoons or more
sugar for sprinkling

*Papayas are always available and usually very inexpensive at the various farmers' markets around the Big Island. They are cheapest on the east side of the island. Papayas are 'ono simply sliced as part of breakfast and are great in green salads (when green) or in fruit salads (when ripe). They can also be made into tasty salsas, jams, marmalades, and desserts.*

*Misty Inouye won the grand prize at the 11th Annual Taste of Puna Cook-off with this rich papaya dessert.*

Place a 9 x 13-inch pan filled with about 3½ cups water in the oven and start the oven preheating to 325°F. Prepare the papaya purée by slicing the papaya in half and discarding the seeding. Scoop the papaya meat into a blender or food processor. Pulse it for 15 seconds or so, long enough to purée the papaya.

Slice open the vanilla bean and scrape the seeds from the pod. Combine the seeds, heavy cream, sugar, and salt in a saucepot. Bring the cream mixture to a boil and then remove it from the heat. Add the lemon zest and the papaya purée to the cream mixture and whisk to mix. Set aside.

Put the egg yolks into a medium-size bowl. Whisk the egg yolks. Then, slowly pour the cream and papaya mixture into the beaten yolks, whisking as you pour. Strain the resulting mixture through a fine sieve. Fill 12 (6 ounce) oven-proof ramekins three-quarters full of the crème brûlée mixture. Put the ramekins in the water bath in the preheated oven. Bake for 40-55 minutes or until the brûlée is set. Remove ramekins from baking pan. Repeat the process for the remaining 12 ramekins. Cool the crème brûlée at room temperature for 30 minutes.

Refrigerate the desserts a minimum of 3 hours or preferably overnight. Place ¼ teaspoon or more of sugar atop of each crème brûlée. Carefully fan a kitchen torch over the surface of the desserts to caramelize the sugar. If you don't have a kitchen torch, you can place the desserts under the broiler and heat them until the sugar caramelizes, or approximately 15 minutes. Enjoy!

*Courtesy of Misty Inouye*

# CHUNKY GUACAMOLE

**MAKES 8 TO 10 SERVINGS**

3 large creamy ripe avocados,
    peeled, seeded, and
    mashed
1 large yellow onion, diced
2 large Granny Smith apples,
    peeled, coarsely chopped
2 large cloves garlic, minced
1½ cups raisins
1 cup bottled sliced jalapeño
    pepper, finely chopped
1 tablespoon lemon juice
    (approximately half of a
    lemon; Meyer lemons are
    the best)
1 teaspoon seasoned salt
½ teaspoon cayenne pepper

*Many varieties of avocado grow on the Big Island, varieties that flower and bear fruit at different times. Chances are good that avocado will always be available at any one of the farmers' markets around the island.*

*If you have an avocado tree on your property you may find that it produces more avocados than you can possibly use. During my "small kid days" we often mashed avocados and mixed them with sugar. A favorite snack was this sweet mixture spread on Saloon Pilot crackers.*

*Here is a recipe for chunky guacamole that uses three large, Big Island avocados. Three down and a few hundred more to go!*

I'm giving the quantities a bit loosely here. Avocados, onions, and apples range in size. You can vary this recipe to taste. If the apple is small and you'd like a little more of it in your guacamole, cut up another and add bits until you get a balance you like.

Mix all the ingredients together in a large bowl. Lomi or massage the guacamole to mix all the flavors. Serve chilled or at room temperature, with tortilla chips.

# MANGO CRACK SEED

### MAKES 1 GALLON

1 gallon cut-up small green
　　mangoes, cut in half right
　　through the seed

### PICKLING SOLUTION

1 gallon water
1 cup salt

### SEASONING

1 pound brown sugar
2 cups sugar
½ cup water
¼ cup lemon juice
1 tablespoon salt
2 teaspoons Chinese five-
　　spice powder

*There is nothing finer than mangoes in season. Picked green, they can be used for Thai salad, pickled, or made into "crack seed." Ripe mangoes can also be made into pies, bread, and salsa, or used as a topping for mango cheesecake.*

*This mango crack seed reminds me of "small kid time."*

Cut up the green mangoes, put them in a gallon jar, and cover them with the pickling solution. Leave the mangoes overnight.

The next day, drain the mangoes and arrange them in one layer on a tray. Put the tray in the hot sun for two days, or until the mango pieces are partly dry.

Bring the brown sugar, sugar, water, lemon juice, five-spice powder, and salt to boil in a large pot. Boil the seasoning until the sugar has dissolved. Add the partly dried mangoes and simmer for 25 minutes. The mangoes should be tender but still firm. Most of the liquid should have evaporated. Pack the mangoes into sterilized jars and seal while hot.

This crack seed can be eaten immediately. It will keep for months, still sealed, in the cupboard.

# POHĀ BERRY JAM

## POHĀ BERRY SAUCE

¼ cup minced shallots

2 teaspoons four-peppercorn-blend (a mixture of red, green, white, and black peppercorns)

1 tablespoon butter

½ cup brandy

1 cup Pohā berries

1½ cups red wine

¼ cup honey

½ cup Pohā berry jam

2 cups veal or beef stock

2 tablespoons cornstarch with 4 tablespoons water to make a slurry

*You can often buy Pohā berries, or cape gooseberries, at our local farmers' markets. Sometimes the berries are sold in their husks, while at other times you can buy just the berries, husked and sold in small, re-sealable bags.*

*Great on toast.*

To make a Pohā berry jam, wash the Pohā berries. Measure the berries, then add an equal amount of sugar. For example, if you have 2 cups of berries, add 2 cups of sugar. Boil the jam until the temperature is at 221 degrees, measured with a candy thermometer, then immediately remove from the heat. This should take about 30 minutes. However, you should be watching the thermometer, not the clock. 221 degrees? Off!

Pour the jam into sterilized jars, leaving a ¼-inch (or larger) headspace between the surface of the jam and the top of the jar. Seal with sterilized canning lids and screw bands.

# POHĀ BERRY SAUCE

*You can use the jam you just made in this tasty sauce, which is great with beef, chicken, or pork.*

**To prepare Pohā Berry Sauce:** Heat the butter in a medium-size saucepan over medium heat. Sauté the shallots and peppercorns until the shallots are translucent. Remove the pan from the heat and pour the brandy into the pan. Return the pan to the heat for one minute.

Now you need to burn off the alcohol in the brandy, leaving the flavors behind. If you are using a gas stove, you can just tilt the saucepan towards the flame; the fumes from the brandy will catch on fire, followed by the rest of the brandy. If you aren't using a gas stove, you'll have to light a match and just touch the surface of the butter and brandy mixture.

Stir in the Pohā berries, red wine, jam, and honey; boil the sauce until it thickens. Add the stock, bring the sauce to a boil again, and cook until the sauce is reduced by half. You will need to keep an eye on the sauce, scraping down the sides of the pan and occasionally stirring. If you want a thicker sauce, you can add cornstarch slurry (1 tablespoon cornstarch mixed with 1 tablespoon cold water). Mix the slurry into the sauce and cook until thick. When the sauce is done, take it off the heat and cover it to keep it warm.

**To serve with meat:** Spoon some sauce onto the serving plate, then put the cooked meat on the sauce. Drizzle some sauce over the top of the beef, chicken, or pork.

# CHAPTER 7

# BIG ISLAND OMIYAGE

OMIYAGE is a Japanese tradition. Anyone traveling to a distant town or province was expected to bring back some of the special foods from that place as treats for family and friends. Today, many Hawai'i residents buy omiyage for friends and family, whether they are Japanese-American or not. If you are visiting the Big Island, what should you buy as omiyage? You have lots of choices—enough to fill a suitcase. You may even want to bring back a "Hawaiian suitcase": a big cooler full of 'ono local foods, taped and roped shut.

If you're traveling to the mainland, and bringing the taste of the Islands to exiled family and friends, you may want to buy:

Kālua pork
Laulau
Pipikaula
Portuguese sausage
Dried 'ōpelu
Smoked marlin or 'ahi
Sakura boshi marlin or 'ahi
'Alaea salt
WOW seasoning

Boiled peanuts (regular or vinegar)
Ogo namasu
Picked radish
Whole takuan
Whole sanbai-zuke
Cookie Nuggets (peanut butter, shortbread, chocolate chip, Kona coffee, just to name a few)
'Ōhelo berry and mulberry preserves

Chili pepper jelly
Kea'au ground coffee
Eurasia dressing
Chichi mochi, an mochi, and other varieties of mochi (only at Hilo stores)
Leis
Anthuriums

Just be sure to pack everything well. If you're going to be taking a long flight, you may want to avoid the most perishable items. If home is one of the other Hawaiian islands, you'll probably be able to get most items at your own local supermarket. For a true Big Island treat, you may want to buy items like: dried 'ōpelu, smoked marlin or 'ahi, sakura boshi (marlin or 'ahi), 'ōhelo berry or mulberry preserves, or Kea'au ground coffee.

# 'AHI SAKURA BOSHI

**MAKES 25 SERVINGS**

15 pounds 'ahi, cut into ¼ x 2
x 4-inch strips

**MARINADE**

4 cups soy sauce

4 cups somen tsuyu (bottled
somen soup base)

4 cups sugar

1 pound brown sugar
(1 regular box)

½ cup sesame oil

½ cup mirin (rice wine for
cooking)

¼ teaspoon fresh ground
Hawaiian chili pepper or
crushed red pepper

2 teaspoons grated fresh
ginger

1 tablespoon mashed garlic
(approximately 6 garlic
cloves)

**GARNISH**

½ cup or more roasted white
sesame seeds

## SUISAN FISH MARKET

Hilo's Suisan Fish Market was founded in 1907 by Waiakea fishermen and fishmongers who sold their fish in Hilo. Eventually the Fish Market moved into a large building that hosted a daily fish auction. The auction building withstood the 1946 and 1960 tsunamis, but was finally closed in 2001 when its owners chose not to comply with FDA regulations. The colorful fish auctions, once a tourist attraction, are a thing of the past. Fortunately, the Suisan Fish Company still operates a retail fish market where you can buy some delectable omiyage.

*One of my Suisan favorites is sakura boshi, or marinated strips of dried 'ahi. It reminds me a little of pipikaula, the paniolo (Hawaiian cowboy) dried beef. If you'd like to try making your own sakura boshi, here's a recipe.*

Mix all the marinade ingredients. Put the fish in a container with a cover and pour the marinade over it. Put in the refrigerator and marinate the fish overnight. Stir at least once to be sure that all the fish is well marinated. The fish on top may be too dry unless you make sure that it takes its turn on the bottom of the container. Drain the excess marinade from the fish.

If you have a dehydrator, leave the fish in the dehydrator until dry. If you don't own one, put the fish in an oven heated to 175°F for 3 or more hours. When the fish is close to completely dry, sprinkle the tops of the 'ahi slices with sesame seeds.

*Courtesy of Suisan Fish Market*

# CRISPY RICE COOKIES

**MAKES 60 COOKIES**

14 ounces butter
   (3½ regular sticks)
1 cup sugar
1½ teaspoons vanilla extract
3 cups flour
1¾ teaspoons baking soda
2 cups rice cereal (crispy
   type)
1 (12 ounce) package
   chocolate chips

## MOUNTAIN VIEW BAKERY

Shigeru Kotomori opened the Mountain View Bakery in 1936. Today the bakery is run by his granddaughter, Lori Sueda (née Kotomori), and her husband, Riley Sueda, along with his great-grandchildren, Riley and Aisha Sueda. The bakery is famous for its stone cookies.

You won't see the Mountain View Bakery if you zip past on Highway 11. The bakery is on the old road. Once you're on the old road, however, you can't miss the bakery, which is painted a glowing yellow. It's open on Monday through Friday from 7:30 a.m. to 1:00 p.m., on Saturday from 7:30 a.m. to 1:30 p.m., and is closed on Sunday.

*Grandpa Shigeru perfected the stone cookie recipe after many years of experimentation. Today you can buy chocolate chip, raisin, coconut, and soft or extra-crispy stone cookies. Although this recipe is a family secret, Lori was willing to share a recipe for her grandmother's crispy rice cookies.*

Cream the butter, sugar, and vanilla extract. Add the flour and baking soda, then the rice cereal and chocolate chips. You can mix everything but the cereal and chocolate chips with a mixer, but the last two ingredients are perhaps best added by hand and stirred with a spoon.

Drop the cookie batter by teaspoonfuls onto an ungreased cookie sheet. Bake at 325°F for 20 minutes or until golden brown. Cool the cookies on wire racks. Store the cookies in an air-tight container after they have completely cooled.

*Courtesy of Mountain View Bakery*

# 'AHI WASABI POKE

1 pound 'ahi, cut into ½-inch
cubes

¼ teaspoon wasabi oil
(wasabi-infused oil)

¼ teaspoon mirin (rice wine
for cooking)

¼ teaspoon sesame oil

1 tablespoon soy sauce

1 tablespoon somen tsuyu
(bottled soup base)

1 to 2 tablespoons tobiko or
masago (fish roe)

¼ cup sliced green onions

*Here's a delicious poke recipe from Suisan.*

Combine all ingredients. You can increase or decrease the wasabi oil to make
hotter or milder poke.

*Courtesy of Suisan Fish Market*

## SPICY OYSTER SAUCE
'AHI POKE (MAKES 6
SERVINGS)

1 pound 'ahi, cut in ½-inch
cubes

3 tablespoons oyster sauce

1 tablespoon soy sauce

¼ cup sliced green onion

½ cup diced onion (yellow,
white, or red onions are all
OK, but will give different
flavors to your poke)

1 Hawaiian chili pepper,
finely diced

# SPICY OYSTER SAUCE 'AHI POKE

*Here's another Suisan poke recipe.*

Combine all ingredients. You can increase or decrease the chili pepper to make
hotter or milder poke.

*Courtesy of Suisan Fish Market*

# SANBAIZUKE DAIKON

**MAKES 8 TO 10 SERVINGS**

4 cups short grain rice
4 cups water
⅓ cup furikake nori
½ cup diced sanbai-zuke
    (¼-inch dice)
1 package shiofuku kombu

## HONDA FOODS

Be sure to look over the offerings from the Big Island company of Honda Foods. Mr. Honda has been making takuan, cabbage kim chee, cucumber kim chee, and sanbai-zuke since 1986. He uses only locally grown daikon from Waimea and Volcano. I think his pickled daikon is unique—there's nothing like it on any of the other islands. His sanbai-zuke is special because he adds ogo (a variety of seaweed) from Keahole, Kona.

*I like to use his sanbai-zuke daikon to make this layered rice dish is great for potlucks and picnics.*

Wash the rice thoroughly. The Koreans say "wash three times, rinse four times." Add 4 cups water and cook the rice in your rice cooker or rice pot.

Line a 9 x 13-inch cake pan with waxed paper. Spread the shiofuku kombu and furikake nori evenly over bottom. While the rice is still hot, spread half of the cooked rice over the kombu and nori. Lightly press down the rice. Spread the diced sanbai-zuke over the first layer of rice, then cover the sanbai-zuke with the remaining rice. Press the rice down firmly; the layers should stick together and hold their shape.

When the rice is cool, invert the pan over a tray or serving platter. The waxed paper, kombu, and nori will now be on the top. Remove the waxed paper and cut the rice into serving pieces.

# PUNALU'U SWEETBREAD

**MAKES 1 SANDWICH LOAF**

1 cup warm water (100°F)

1 package (2¼ teaspoons)
    active dry yeast

1 package (20.16 ounces)
    Punalu'u Sweetbread Mix

## PUNALU'U BAKE SHOP

Punalu'u Bake Shop in Nā'ālehu is a great place to shop for omiyage if you are traveling around the island. The Bake Shop is known for its sweetbread (pao doçe), which comes in three flavors: traditional, taro (purple bread), and guava (pink bread). They are also famous for their malasadas: traditional, taro, guava, vanilla cream filled, strawberry filled, apple filled, chocolate filled, and liliko'i (passion fruit) glazed. So many choices!

The Bake Shop also sells packages of sweetbread mix. This is an excellent omiyage. It is easy to carry home and doesn't have to be eaten immediately. Be sure to buy extra for yourself so that when the urge for sweetbread or malasadas hits, you can make some on the spot.

Mix the yeast and the water in a large bread bowl or mixing bowl. Let the yeast sit for 5 minutes. Add the bread mix to the yeast and mix well. If you have a heavy-duty stand mixer with a dough hook, you can knead the dough right in the mixing bowl. Knead no more than 10 minutes. The dough should be soft and supple. If you don't have a heavy-duty mixer, you'll have to knead the dough by hand. Place it on a floured board and knead for 10–13 minutes. (See the recipe for Portuguese White Bread, page 24, for kneading instructions.)

Put the dough into a buttered or oiled bowl, cover, and put the bowl in a warm place until the dough has doubled in volume. This should take approximately 1½ to 2 hours.

Punch down the dough, put it into buttered or oiled loaf pans, cover it with a cloth, and let it rise until it has again doubled in size. Bake it at 325°F for 50 minutes. Cool at least 30 minutes before cutting.

(continued on page 178)

(continued from page 177)

*Or, if you'd like, you can use the sweetbread dough to make azuki anpan or char siu bau.*

## AZUKI ANPAN

**MAKES APPROXIMATELY 12 ANPAN**

1 recipe Punaluʻu Bake Shop
   sweetbread (see above),
   risen only once
1 can (18 ounces) koshi-an
   (azuki bean paste)

1) Form the bread dough into 2-inch diameter balls.
2) Flatten them into 5-inch diameter circles.
3) Place 1 tablespoon of koshi-an in the middle of each circle.
4) Pinch the sides of the circle until the dough completely covers the koshi-an.
5) Pinch the dough to seal the anpan.
6) Place the pinched side of the anpan on a cookie sheet or jelly roll pan lined with parchment paper. Cover the anpan with a cloth.

Allow the anpan to rise again until they have doubled in size. This should take approximately 1½ hours.

Preheat the oven to 325°F. Bake the anpan for 20 minutes, or until golden brown.

2 teaspoons canola oil

1 pound char siu, diced (¼-
    inch dice)

1 tablespoon low-sodium
    soy sauce

2 tablespoons regular oyster
    sauce or vegetarian
    mushroom sauce

1 tablespoon sugar

1½ cups chicken broth

2 teaspoons sesame oil

Salt and pepper to taste

### CORNSTARCH SLURRY

2 tablespoons cornstarch
    dissolved in 4 tablespoons
    cold water

# CHAR SIU BAU
# (PORK BUNS OR MANAPUA)

*You can also use the sweet bread dough to make your own char siu bau. Char siu, as I'm sure you know, is Chinese spiced pork. You'll find a recipe for homemade char siu on page 7.*

Heat the oil in a wok or heavy frying pan, then add the char siu, soy sauce, oyster sauce, sugar, chicken broth, and sesame oil. Stir fry the char siu and seasonings until they are well mixed and piping hot. Add the cornstarch slurry and stir until the pan juices thicken. Cool the filling.

Prepare the bau exactly as you prepared the anpan. Divide the dough into 2-inch balls, flatten, add 1 tablespoon of filling, close up, and let rise. Preheat the oven to 325°F. Bake the bau for 20 minutes, or until golden brown.

*Courtesy of Punalu'u Bake Shop*

# CATHY'S FAVORITE MOUSSE CAKE

**MAKES ONE 9-INCH PIE**

**CHOCOLATE TURTLE PLOP COOKIE CRUST**

⅔ cup chopped dry-roasted macadamia nut

2⅔ ounces Original Hawaiian Chocolate Factory Dark Chocolate, melted

⅓ cup unsalted butter (2⅔ ounces, or ⅔ of a regular stick)

¼ cup brown sugar

¼ cup sugar

1 egg

½ teaspoon vanilla (Hawaiian vanilla if possible)

⅔ cup flour

½ teaspoon baking soda

¼ teaspoon salt

⅔ cup chocolate chips (Kailua Candy company "turtle droppings" if you can get them)

## KAILUA CANDY COMPANY

Jack and Jenny Smoot opened the Kailua Candy Company in 1977. Their daughter, Cathy, and her husband, Robin Barrett, eventually joined the business. Today, Cathy and Robin run Kailua Candy Company in Kailua-Kona's Kaloko Industrial Area. They are best known for their macadamia nut caramel-chocolate turtles. They also sell pies, cakes, and assorted candies.

If you're looking for a great omiyage, I can enthusiastically recommend their treats.

Cathy graciously shared with us her recipe for Cathy's Favorite Mousse Cake, which is a customer favorite at her retail store.

*This cake won't taste like Cathy's unless you use all the Original Hawaiian Chocolate Factory products that she uses. But if you can't get them, that's OK too. If you use generic ingredients you'll still have a darn good cake. If you can't get Original Hawaiian Chocolate Factory dark chocolate, use Hershey's Chocolatier or Baker's Bittersweet.*

*This is an elaborate confection that you may not want to make frequently, but it will be a hit whenever you do.*

**To make the crust:** Put the butter in a large mixing bowl and beat until creamy. Gradually add the brown and white sugars; beat until light and fluffy. Add the egg and beat well. Beat in the melted chocolate and vanilla. Stir in the flour, salt, and baking soda. Finally, fold in the chocolate chips (the "turtle droppings"). Line the bottom of a 9-inch diameter springform pan with parchment paper and preheat the oven to 375°F. Scrape the dough into the springform pan and bake for 7-9 minutes. Cool completely. Do not remove the crust from the pan, as you will be pouring the mousse into the pan later.

**To make the cake:** Melt the chocolate in the top half of a double boiler. Pour the melted chocolate into a large bowl and add the brewed coffee; mix the melted chocolate and coffee with a wire whisk until they are completely smooth. Stir in the yolks one at a time.

Whip the egg whites with a whisk or mixer until soft peaks form. Fold the whites into the chocolate-coffee-yolk mixture with a spatula, a flat whisk, or, for maximum delicacy, your hand. Fold, not mix—you have to handle the beaten whites very carefully or you will drive out all the air you just finished beating into the whites.

Whip the cream (no need to clean the mixing bowl and whip). Gently fold the whipped cream into the mousse.

Spray the inside of the springform pan with cooking spray. The baked crust should still be inside the pan. Pour the mousse into the pan, on top of the crust. Refrigerate the cake overnight. This should set the mousse.

**To make the ganache:** When you are ready to ice the mousse cake, you can make the ganache. Heat the cream in the microwave until hot. This should take approximately one minute, depending on the wattage of your microwave. If you are unsure of the wattage or the time needed, heat in short bursts and check the cream between bursts to be sure that it's warm enough. Don't boil the cream.

### GANACHE

2 ounces Original Hawaiian Chocolate Factory Dark Chocolate, melted

2 ounces heavy cream

### CAKE

1 dark chocolate turtle plop cookie crust (see above)

Ganache (see above)

1 pound Original Hawaiian Chocolate Factory's Dark Chocolate

⅔ cup brewed coffee (Cathy uses dark roast peaberry Kona Coffee)

2 eggs, separated

1 cup heavy cream

Melt the 2 ounces of chocolate in the top half of a double boiler, or, if you are brave, in a thick-bottomed pan, stirring constantly. Pour the hot cream over the melted chocolate; stir the ganache gently with a whisk until it is completely smooth.

**To ice the cake:** Carefully remove the cake from the springform pan and place it on a wire rack set over a large plate. Pour the ganache over the mousse cake. You can scrape up any ganache that pools on the plate and pour it over the cake again. When the cake is well covered, put it in the refrigerator. Refrigerate the cake until the ganache topping is firm. You can then carefully slide the cake onto a serving plate.

*Courtesy of Kailua Candy Company*

# PIE CRUST MANJU

¾ pound vegetable
  shortening
1 stick butter
5 cups flour
1 teaspoon salt
1 (18 ounce) can tsubushi
  or koshi-an (azuki
  bean fillings)
¾ cup milk
½ cup evaporated milk,
  to brush on manju
  before baking

## BLUE KALO BRAND

H. Fujii Store and Bakery opened in 1936 and closed when the elderly owners retired. It was a great place to buy six-inch pies, manju, anpan, and cinnamon snails. Sigh. I miss them.

However, I also love Blue Kalo Brand, a business that recently opened in the old H. Fujii Store and Bakery building in Wailea. Aaron and Vinel Sugino, the proprietors, stock wonderful fried chips made from 'ulu (breadfruit), purple sweet potato, yellow sweet potato, and cassava. The chips are perfectly salted and not at all greasy. Blue Kalo also sells local-kine cookies like 'ulu, sweet potato, and coconut crisps, as well as poi cookies with oatmeal or peanut butter. They sell pies and manju too.

You can also find Blue Kalo products in a few retail stores, or buy them at the farmers' market on Kino'ole Street on Saturdays.

*Here is a basic recipe for pie crust manju. You can fill these manju with all kinds of creative fillings, just like the ones at Blue Kalo.*

Cream the shortening, salt, and butter together, then cut the flour into the butter mixture with a pastry cutter or two knives. Add the milk and gently mix until the dough is well combined. Do not mix it into a homogenous paste, or the pie crust wrapper will not be flaky. Form the dough into 1-inch diameter balls (Blue Kalo uses a number 40 scoop to make the balls). Put a ball in your cupped hand and use the other hand to flatten the ball. Put 1 tablespoon of tsubushi or koshi-an in the center of the flattened dough, then close up the manju by stretching and pleating the dough over the filling. Place the manju on a cookie sheet lined with parchment paper, sealed side down.

Preheat your oven to 325°F. Brush the tops of the manju with the evaporated milk. Bake the manju in the preheated oven for 20 minutes, or until brown.

You can also fill the manju with sweet potato an. To make sweet potato an, mix equal parts boiled, mashed sweet potatoes and sugar. That is, for every cup of mashed sweet potatoes, you'd add one cup of sugar. This is a basic recipe for an; you can use it to make 'ulu an, lima bean an, etc.

# 'ULU CHIPS

**MAKES 6 SERVINGS**

1 half-ripe 'ulu (breadfruit)
Oil for deep-frying
Garlic salt

When breadfruit is ripe it's sweet and fruity. Half-ripe 'ulu is still starchy and firm; this is the best kind to use for chips.

*If you have a deep fryer that maintains an even temperature, these chips will be easy. If you are frying in a wok, a big pot, or a deep Dutch oven, be sure to use a deep-frying thermometer to ensure that the oil stays at the proper temperature. That's the key to successful deep-frying.*

Wash the half-ripe 'ulu. Cut off the stem, then cut the 'ulu in half lengthwise. No need to peel. Slice the 'ulu halves as thinly as possible. It's hard to get them thin enough with a knife. A cook's mandoline would be extremely helpful here.

Cover the bottom of a baking pan or cookie sheet with paper towels. Heat the deep-frying oil to 350°F.

Slide a few 'ulu chips at a time into the heated oil and fry. The chips will turn light brown when they are done; this should take about 3 minutes.

Put the cooked chips into the towel-lined pan and sprinkle them with garlic salt. To remove any grease left over from the deep-frying, you can leave the chips on the towels until the towels have soaked up the grease. You might also try putting the cooked chips in a salad spinner and spinning them to remove the oil.

# CHICHI MOCHI

**MAKES APPROXIMATELY
54 SLICES OF MOCHI**

4 cups mochiko (sweet rice
  flour)

3 cups sugar

1 (13½ ounce) can coconut
  milk

A few drops of red food
  coloring to turn the
  mixture pink

2 cups water

1½ teaspoons white miso

## TWO LADIES KITCHEN

Nora Uchida and Aunty Tomi Tokeshi opened the Two Ladies Kitchen in 1996. Aunty Tomi has retired, but Nora and her crew are still running a very successful mochi and manju business.

*This chichi mochi recipe is Nora's favorite; she got it from her girlfriend, Beverly Takemoto. It contains 1½ teaspoons of white miso, which is an unusual twist on the staple recipe.*

Mix all ingredients well. Grease a 9 x 13-inch baking pan. Pour the mochi mixture into the pan and cover the pan tightly with foil. Bake in a 325°F oven for 1 hour.

Remove the mochi from the oven and let it cool. When it is completely cooled, invert the pan to turn the mochi onto a surface coated with katakuriko or potato starch.

Cut the mochi into 1 x 2-inch slices. Cut 5 x 5-inch squares of waxed paper. Put the mochi pieces in the center of the paper, bring together two diagonally-opposite corners of the paper, and twist them to close the wrapper.

*Courtesy of Beverly Takemoto*

# SWEET NUTS AND BOLTS

1 large box of corn square
    cereal

1 large box rice square cereal

1 box honeycomb type
    cereal

1 large bag corn chips

1 bag bugle shaped snacks

1 bag cheese puffs

## SAVORY SAUCE

4 sticks butter

1 cup sugar

1 teaspoon garlic powder

1 tablespoon Worcestershire
    sauce

## BIG ISLAND DELIGHTS

Carla and Jeff Takamine opened a retail store in 1996. At first they only sold goodies from other suppliers, but in 1997 they began to bake and sell their own cookies. These cookies were such a hit that the Takamines were soon supplying them to other stores. Today most of their business is wholesale. Carla and Jeff have recruited many relatives to help them out with their growing business; several generations of Yamagatas and Takamines are now working together to bring us their wonderful goodies.

*I happen to like their snack mixes. I asked for the recipe for one of my favorites and they were kind enough to share it.*

Melt the butter in a large and deep baking or roasting pan. Add the sugar, garlic powder, and Worcestershire sauce and mix well. Preheat the oven to 250°F and heat the savory sauce until the sugar melts and the sauce thickens.

Pull the pan out of the oven and add all the cereals, chips, and puffs. Mix everything well so that the "nuts and bolts" are well coated with the sugar mixture. Put the pan back into the oven and bake for 1 hour. Turn the mix every 15 minutes to be sure all is mixed well and cooks evenly.

*Courtesy of Big Island Delights*

# SUGARCANE SWEET

# CHAPTER 8

THE Big Island is a great place for dessert cooks who like to use fresh local ingredients. The last of our sugar plantations closed in 1996, but our island is still home to cultivated fruits like guava, Waimea strawberries, liliko'i (passion fruit), mangoes, banana, pohā berries, and papaya. The wild 'ōhelo berry grows in our uplands. We also grow coconuts, macadamia nuts, and vanilla for vanilla extract. With a little bit of imagination and local ingredients, you can create some toothsome desserts.

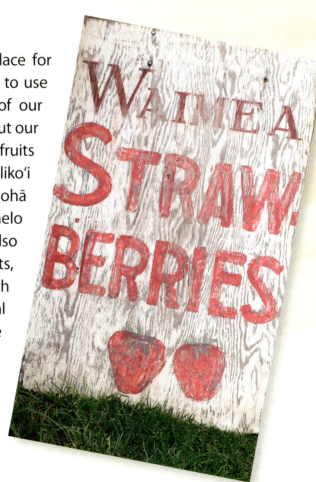

# MACADAMIA NUT STICKY BUNS

**MAKES 12 BUNS**

## DOUGH

1¼ cups warm water

½ cup honey

1½ teaspoons active dry yeast

1 large egg, room temperature

1 tablespoon vegetable oil

1½ teaspoons salt

19 ounces all-purpose flour (by weight; use a kitchen scale)

4 ounces cake flour (by weight)

## TOPPING

1 cup unsalted butter, softened

1 cup light brown sugar

## CINNAMON SUGAR

½ cup sugar

1 tablespoon ground cinnamon

## EGG WASH

1 large egg, beaten

## GARNISH

1 cup chopped macadamia nuts

## SHORT N SWEET BAKERY & CAFE

If you find yourself in Hāwī, Kohala, you might want to stop by the Short N Sweet Bakery & Café. Maria Short, the owner, worked as the pastry chef for the Kukio Golf and Beach Club before she left to start her own café. I love her baked goods and her lunch specials.

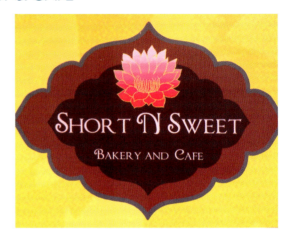

*She was kind enough to share her recipe for macadamia nut sticky buns. These are great for breakfast; in fact, they're great any time you have a snack attack!*

**To prepare the dough:** Combine the warm water and the honey in a large bread bowl. Sprinkle the yeast over the water and honey; let the mixture stand until the yeast has softened. Add the egg and the oil to the yeast/honey mixture. Sift or whisk together the flour and salt and add them to the wet ingredients. Mix until a loose dough forms; the dough will be sticky. Cover the bowl with plastic wrap and let the dough rise until it doubles in size. After one rising, punch down the dough and refrigerate it while you are making the topping.

**To make the topping:** Mix the butter and brown sugar together until just combined (do not cream mixture). Spread the butter/brown sugar mixture evenly into the bottom of a 9 x 13-inch baking pan.

**To make the cinnamon sugar:** Stir the sugar and cinnamon together in a small bowl until they are completely blended and there are no lumps.

**To form the buns:** Pat the dough into a 10 x 12-inch rectangle on a well-floured surface. Lightly brush the surface of the dough with the egg wash and liberally sprinkle with cinnamon sugar.

Starting with the long side of the dough rectangle, roll the dough into a log, as you would roll a jelly roll. Cut the resulting log into 12 slices.

Press one-twelfth of the chopped macadamia nuts into the top of each slice. Put the buns into the butter/brown sugar lined pan, NUT SIDE DOWN. Be sure to leave some room around each bun.

Let the buns rise again until they touch each other and have risen more than half-way up the sides of the pan.

**To bake:** Bake at 350°F until the tops of the buns are golden brown. The brown sugar and butter on the bottom of the pan will caramelize; you should see the caramel bubbling around the edges of the pan. While the buns are still hot, invert pan very carefully to slide the buns out onto a serving platter. (If you wait until the buns cool, the caramel will stick to the pan. If you aren't careful, you might splash yourself with boiling caramel.)

Let the buns cool a bit before eating.

*Courtesy of Short N Sweet Bakery & Cafe*

# 'ŌHELO BERRY CREAM CHEESE PIE

**MAKES ONE 9-INCH PIE**

### PIE TOPPING

3 cups 'ōhelo berries

2 cups sugar

2 tablespoons lemon juice

¾ + ¼ cup water

2 tablespoons cornstarch

### PIE CRUST

½ cup (1 regular stick) butter

¼ cup brown sugar

1 cup all-purpose white flour

½ cup chopped macadamia
    nuts

### PIE FILLING

1 (8 ounce) package cream
    cheese, room temperature

1 teaspoon vanilla extract
    (Hawaiian if possible)

½ cup powdered sugar

1 (8 ounce) container Cool
    Whip whipped topping

*'Ōhelo berries grow high up on the slopes of our volcanoes. They grow especially well in and near the town of Volcano, where I live, and are sacred to the Hawaiian volcano goddess, Pele. We don't pick berries in Volcanoes National Park, as the berries are a prime food supply for the endangered nēnē geese living in the park. However, these lovely berries grow outside the park too. When they're in season, there is nothing finer than fresh 'ōhelo berries! I think they make a lovely pie; try it and see if you agree with me.*

**To make the pie topping:** Mix the berries, sugar, lemon juice, and ¾ cup water in a medium-size pot. Bring the topping to a boil over medium heat, then remove it from the heat. Mix the 2 tablespoons of cornstarch with ¼ cup cold water, then slowly add the cornstarch mixture to the topping, stirring as you add. The topping should thicken without cornstarch lumps. When the topping has cooled to room temperature, put it into a covered container and store it in the refrigerator. It must be completely cool before you can spoon it over the top of the pie.

**To make the pie crust:** Put the cold butter, flour, and brown sugar in a large bowl. Using two knives or a pastry cutter, cut the butter into tiny pieces. Mix well, add the chopped macadamia nuts, and mix again. Press the mixture into a 9-inch pie pan, making sure that it's of even thickness all over. Bake at 350°F for 15 minutes, or until the pie crust is golden brown. Cool before filling.

**To make the pie filling:** Using a stand mixer, hand mixer, or just a wooden spoon, mix the cream cheese and powdered sugar until the cream cheese is light and fluffy. Add the vanilla extract and mix again. Carefully fold the whipped topping into the cream cheese mixture.

**To assemble:** Spoon the cream cheese mixture into the baked pie crust; level the filling with a spatula if necessary. Pour the 'ōhelo berry topping over the top of the pie. You can serve this immediately, or chill it in the refrigerator until it is to be served.

# RICH VANILLA ICE CREAM

## TROPICAL DREAMS

Tropical Dreams has been making gourmet ice cream on the Big Island for over twenty years. They make twenty-five different flavors of ice cream, ten flavors of sorbet, and three of frozen yogurt; they sell to over eighty vendors throughout the state of Hawai'i.

*Nancy Edney, one of the owners, shared this vanilla ice cream recipe. This ice cream is luscious all by itself, and spectacular when flavored with optional ingredients such as chopped macadamia nuts, chopped chocolate cookies, or minced candied ginger.*

Whisk or beat the egg yolks, ¼ cup sugar, and salt in a medium-size bowl until the mixture is thick and pale yellow.

Combine the milk, cream, vanilla bean and seeds, and the remaining ¼ cup sugar in a heavy saucepan. Cook over medium heat until the milk and cream just start to bubble. Remove from the heat. Slowly pour the milk and cream mixture into the egg mixture, whisking as you pour. If you pour too quickly, or don't mix well, the heat of the milk and cream may curdle the eggs, resulting in "scrambled eggs."

Return the egg/milk/cream mixture to the saucepan and cook over medium-low heat, stirring constantly with a heat-resistant spatula or a metal whisk. Use a candy thermometer to check the heat; you should cook only until the custard reaches 175°F. It should lightly coat the spatula. Don't let the custard boil or the eggs will scramble.

Strain the custard into a clean bowl and discard the vanilla bean. Cool in an ice bath. (Put the bowl into a larger bowl filled with ice cubes and ice water; this quickly cools the custard.) When the custard has cooled to room temperature, cover the bowl and refrigerate the custard for 4 hours or longer.

Churn the custard in an ice cream machine according to the manufacturer's instructions. Result: delicious ice cream. Any leftover ice cream should be stored in the freezer.

*Courtesy of Tropical Dreams*

### MAKES 6 SERVINGS

6 large egg yolks
¼ + ¼ cup sugar
Pinch of salt
1½ cups whole milk
2½ cups heavy whipping cream
1 teaspoon pure vanilla extract (Hawaiian if possible)
1 vanilla bean, cut in half and seeds scraped out

# CASCARON OR FILIPINO FRIED DOUGHNUT

**MAKES 24 CASCARONS**

1 pound mochiko

1¼ cups sugar

¾ tablespoon baking powder

¼ cup coconut milk

Sesame seeds

Water

Canola oil for deep frying

*Okinawans make andagi, the Portuguese make malasadas, and the Filipinos make cascaron. Cascaron doughnuts are deliciously chewy because they are made with mochiko, or rice flour.*

Mix the mochiko, sugar, and baking powder; add the coconut milk and mix. The dough should be thick enough to shape into 1-inch diameter balls. If it's too dry to shape, add just enough water to make a dough you can handle.

Form all the dough into the 1-inch balls. Roll the cascaron balls in the sesame seeds, then flatten them slightly with your hand. You will probably want to lay them out on a towel, a cookie sheet, or a strip of waxed paper.

Fill a heavy pot or deep skillet with canola oil to a depth of 1 inch. Heat the oil to 325°F. Fry the cascaron on both sides, then transfer to a paper towel.

Serve the cascaron when they have cooled enough to eat.

# FRESH WAIMEA STRAWBERRY TART

MAKES ONE 9 X 13-INCH TART

## CRUST

2 cups flour

1 cup (2 regular sticks) butter

¼ cup sifted powdered sugar

## FILLING

3 cups sugar

½ cup cornstarch

5 cups boiling water

1 (6 ounces) large or 2 (3 ounces) small strawberry flavored gelatin dessert.

2 teaspoons vanilla extract (Hawaiian if possible)

1 package (¼ ounce) unflavored gelatin

1 tablespoon cold water

3 pounds (three 16-ounce plastic fruit baskets) fresh Waimea strawberries

*To me, there is nothing sweeter and more delicious than Waimea strawberries in season. This Waimea strawberry tart recipe brings out the best in our locally grown strawberries.*

**To make the crust:** Mix the flour, butter, and powdered sugar with two knives or a pastry cutter; it should be well mixed and crumbly. Butter and flour a 9 x 13-inch pan. (I like to use Baker's Joy, which is a butter and flour spray that prepares the pan quickly and easily. However, you can also prepare the pan the old-fashioned way.) Press the crust mixture into the pan, forming an even layer. Bake the crust in a 350°F oven for 15 minutes, or until the crust is golden brown. Cool it to room temperature before adding the filling.

**To make the filling:** Place the cornstarch in cold water, heat on medium, and stir constantly until the mixture thickens. Add strawberry gelatin.

Mix the unflavored gelatin with the tablespoon of cold water and let sit for 5 minutes or so. The gelatin should "bloom," or thicken. When the unflavored gelatin has bloomed, mix the sugar, cornstarch with strawberry gelatin mixture, and the unflavored gelatin in a large mixing bowl. Slowly add the 5 cups of boiling water, mixing as you pour. Whisk until there are no lumps, then allow the filling to cool.

While the filling is cooling, you can prepare the strawberries. Wash them well and remove all the green stems and leaves. Lay out the strawberries on a paper towel or lint-free kitchen towel and pat them with another towel to dry them. Cut the larger strawberries in half, and leave the rest whole. If there are any berries with parts that are too green and tart, or too ripe and spoiled, to eat, you can trim and halve them, or you can set them aside for snacking.

**To assemble:** Gently pour the filling into the crust, then add the strawberries. The strawberries will sink into the filling. Make sure that the strawberries are evenly distributed over the crust; you don't want a lump of strawberry in the center and nothing on the edges. Refrigerate the tart until the filling has set. You may want to save some of the prettier strawberries to garnish the top of the tart.

# BANANA CREAM PIE

**MAKES ONE 9-INCH DIAMETER PIE**

**SERVES 6-8**

2 cups sliced bananas
1 baked 9-inch pie shell

**CUSTARD**
4 large eggs
3 cups evaporated milk
½ cup sugar
½ cup cornstarch
1 teaspoon Hawaiian vanilla
    extract
1 teaspoon lemon extract

Whether you grow apple bananas in your backyard or buy them, banana cream pie is a great way to eat them.

*There are two schools of thought about banana cream pie. Some people like their pie with whipped cream; some people like to top the pie with a meringue. I like a meringue-topped pie myself, so that's the recipe I'm giving here. The meringue is what is called an "Italian" meringue, made with hot sugar syrup. It's a little tricky, but it holds up well to Big Island humidity. If you don't want to bother with the meringue, you can leave it off and just top the pie with whipped cream. In that case, save the egg whites in the refrigerator (they will hold for four days) and use them for angel food cake or macaroons.*

Separate the eggs. Set the egg whites aside, or put them in the refrigerator if you are not going to make a meringue topping. Beat the egg yolks with a fork or whisk.

**To make the custard:** Mix together the milk, sugar, and cornstarch in a heavy pot. Cook the mixture over low heat till thick, stirring constantly with a wire whisk. Take the pot off the heat while you add the egg yolks.

Add a dollop of the hot cornstarch mixture to the bowl of egg yolks and mix well. Then slowly pour the yolk mixture into the cornstarch mixture, stirring all the time. Return the pot to the heat and cook for another 5 minutes.

As the yolks cook, what is now a custard mixture will thicken even further. You must stir constantly, or the egg yolks will harden into fragments of scrambled egg.

## MERINGUE

½ cup egg whites at room
    temperature
¼ teaspoon cream of tartar
1 cup sugar
2 tablespoons corn syrup
¼ cup water

When the custard is done, there will be no more foam on the edges of the pot and the mixture will be very thick. Remove from heat. Add the vanilla and lemon extract and mix well.

**To make the meringue:** Put the ½ cup of egg whites and the cream of tartar in the mixing bowl for your stand mixer. (You can also make the meringue with a hand-held mixer, but you may need someone to help you; one person to heat the sugar syrup and one person to whip the egg whites.)

In a heavy pot over medium heat, heat the sugar, corn syrup, and water. Cook until the temperature reaches 240°F (use a candy thermometer). At this point, start beating the egg whites. Continue heating the sugar mixture till it reaches 250°F. While the mixer is running, slowly pour the sugar mixture into the egg whites. Be careful; the mixture is very hot. This hot mixture will "cook" the whites and make a very stiff, stable meringue that will not shrink.

**To assemble the pie:** Slice bananas onto the bottom of the baked pie shell. Spoon the custard over the bananas, then spread the meringue over the custard. Spread from the outside in; the meringue needs to be firmly anchored to the edges of the pie shell. Bake the finished pie in an oven heated to 350°F for 20 minutes, turning once or twice to be sure that the meringue is evenly browned.

If you aren't making the meringue, you can slice some more bananas over the top of the pie, swirl some whipped cream on top, and serve. Good even without whipped cream.

# HAWAIIAN OGO CARROT CAKE

**MAKES 24 SERVINGS**

2 cups fresh Royal Hawaiian
  Sea Farms long red ogo,
  rinsed and finely chopped
2 cups carrots, grated
1 cup shredded coconut
1 cup crushed pineapple,
  drained
1½ cups vegetable oil
2 cups sugar
4 eggs
2½ cups flour
1 teaspoon baking soda
1 teaspoon baking powder
2 teaspoons ground
  cinnamon

**BUTTER CREAM FROSTING**

4 ounces cream cheese
¼ cup butter
1 teaspoon vanilla extract
1 cup powdered sugar

*Who would think of putting ogo (a thin, crunchy red seaweed) in a cake? Big Islanders would! Hawaiian Sea Farms created this innovative carrot cake, enriched with two cups of ogo.*

**To prepare the cake:** Mix oil, sugar, and eggs until well combined. Stir in ogo, carrots, coconut, and pineapple. Mix or sift the dry ingredients together and gradually add them to the batter, stirring as you add. Pour the batter into a greased and floured 9 x 13-inch pan. Bake at 350°F for 45-50 minutes. Serve plain or with butter cream frosting.

**To prepare the frosting:** Combine the cream cheese and butter and mix until smooth. Add the vanilla and powdered sugar and mix again. Spread the frosting on the cooled cake.

*Courtesy of Royal Hawaiian Sea Farms*

# GRAND MARNIER® SOUFFLÉ

MAKES 4 SOUFFLÉS

**BATTER**

½ cup whole milk
¼ cup sugar
1 teaspoon finely chopped
  orange zest
3 ounces unsalted butter
5 tablespoons bread flour
3 eggs, separated
1½ tablespoons Grand
  Marnier®

**MERINGUE**

3 egg whites
Pinch cream of tartar
1 tablespoon sugar
4 (6-ounce) soufflé cups

*This soufflé is a best seller at the Mauna Kea Resort. It combines the complex flavors of Grand Marnier® liqueur with an intense, citrus tang.*

**To prepare the soufflé base:** Bring the milk and sugar to a boil, while stirring constantly. When they have boiled (be sure not to let the milk boil over onto the stove), remove the milk from the heat.

Melt the butter in a separate pot, making sure the pot is large enough to hold the boiled milk as well as the butter. Add the flour to the melted butter. Cook the flour in the butter for a few minutes; if you don't, the soufflé will taste of flour. However, you also have to be careful not to cook the roux, or butter and flour mixture, for too long. Don't let the roux darken.

Slowly add the boiled milk mixture to the roux, stirring constantly with a whisk to remove any lumps. Cook for one minute, just until the soufflé base thickens. Remove the soufflé base from the heat and allow it to cool. When the mixture has cooled to the point that it is still slightly warm, but not room temperature, slowly add the beaten egg yolks and mix well.

**To prepare the soufflé cups:** Butter and sprinkle with sugar four (6 ounce) soufflé cups. Set the oven temperature to 375°F.

**To prepare the meringue:** Whip the egg whites with the cream of tartar and a little of the sugar. When the whites begin to foam, slowly add the rest of the sugar. Whip the whites to soft peaks.

**To mix the soufflé:** Fold a portion of the meringue into the soufflé batter with the orange zest and 1 tablespoon of Grand Marnier®. Fold in the rest of the meringue.

**To bake:** Place ½ tablespoon Grand Marnier® in the cup before filling with soufflé mixture and fill three-fourths full. Bake in the middle of the preheated 375°F oven for 25 minutes or until soufflé is just set. (Your oven might actually be hotter or cooler than the number on the dial; it might also have a hot spot or two. As this soufflé requires even, exact heat, you may have to adjust your oven temperature slightly or position the soufflé outside the hot spot. You can check your oven temperature with an oven thermometer.)

*Courtesy of Chef Ross Alaimo, Mauna Kea Resorts*

# LILIKOʻI CHIFFON PIE

**MAKES ONE 9-INCH PIE**

1 package (¼ ounce)
unflavored gelatin

¼ cup cold water

4 large eggs, separated

½ + ½ cup sugar

½ cup pure lilikoʻi juice
(thawed if you have
frozen it)

½ teaspoon salt

1 (9-inch) baked pie shell (see
the recipe for ʻŌhelo Berry
Cream Cheese Pie, page
191, or buy ready-made
shells)

½ cup whipped heavy cream

*Lilikoʻi, or passion fruit, grows on a climbing vine (Passiflora edulis var. flavicarpa) that likes to twine over fencing and trellises. It grows well on the Big Island. If you are lucky enough to have these vines on your property you will likely be blessed with an abundance of fruit during the summer months. What to do with it all? I juice and freeze it in ½-cup portions, just right for making this delicious pie. My family can then enjoy our summer bounty year round.*

To extract the juices, place the pulp and seeds in a blender and pulse for 3 seconds. This should separate the seeds from the pulp. Strain the juice from the pulp and seeds. I put the juice, divided into ½-cup portions, into resealable plastic bags, and freeze the bags. Sprinkle the gelatin over the cold water and stir to dissolve. Allow the gelatin to sit for 5 minutes. It will "bloom," or thicken.

Beat the egg yolks until they are frothy. Combine the beaten yolks, ½ cup sugar, the lilikoʻi juice, and salt in a double boiler. Cook the lilikoʻi custard over boiling water until it is thick and smooth, stirring constantly so the eggs do not scramble. Remove the custard from the heat and stir in the gelatin. Cover the pot and refrigerate it until the lilikoʻi custard begins to set.

While the lilikoʻi custard is cooling, beat the egg whites with a stand or hand mixer. Gradually add the last ½ cup sugar to the whites, whipping them until they form stiff peaks. Fold the egg whites into the chilled lilikoʻi custard mixture, then pour the pie filling into the baked pie shell. Chill the pie until the filling is set.

***To serve:*** Garnish wedges of pie with the whipped cream.

# GLOSSARY

**Aburage**—twice-fried slices of tofu; fried bean curd

**Achiote Seeds**—seeds from the lipstick plant, also called annatto or achuete

**'Ahi**—yellowfin tuna

**Aku**—skipjack tuna

**Alae Salt**—Hawaii salt mixed with red clay

**Andagi**—Okinawan doughnut

**Arborio Rice**—Italian medium-grain rice used in risotto

**Awamori**—distilled Okinawan rice wine

**Azuki Beans**—dark red beans

**Bau**—Chinese bun

**Bok Choy**—a type of cabbage used in Chinese cuisine

**Char Siu**—roasted sweet red pork

**Chop Suey Vegetables**—a mixture of vegetables like sliced carrots, celery, onions, jicama, and mung bean sprouts

**Coconut Syrup**—syrup made from coconut milk

**Chinese Five-Spice Powder**—blend of star anise, cloves, fennel, peppercorns, and cinnamon

**Daikon**—long white radish or turnip

**Dashi No Moto**—powdered soup stock base

**Furikake**—Japanese seasoned seaweed mix, used as rice condiment

**Gobo**—burdock root

**Haupia**—Hawaiian coconut pudding

**Hawaiian Red Pepper**—small, spicy red chili pepper

**Hawaiian Salt**—coarse sea salt

**Hoisin Sauce**—Chinese spicy miso-based sauce

**Ichiban Dashi**—basic Japanese soup stock, also used in ponzu sauce

**Imu**—underground pit that uses hot stones to cook food

**'Inamona**—roasted, pounded, and salted kikui nut

**Japanese Vinegar**—rice vinegar, milder than white vinegar

**Kālua**—traditional Hawaiian cooking method using an underground pit called an imu

**Kalbi**—Korean barbecued short ribs

**Kakuma**—hāpu'u fern shoots, often boiled then soaked in water to remove any sap

**Kamaboko**—steamed fish cake, usually on a stick, shaped like a half moon

**Kamatis**—Filipino word for tomatoes

**Kamote**—sweet potato and its leaves used in Filipino cuisine

**Katsuo-boshi**—dried bonito shavings

**Kim Chee**—Korean spicy pickled vegetables

**Ko Choo Jung**—Korean sauce made from mochi rice and chili peppers

**Kombu**—dried kelp

**Konnyaku**—tuber root flour cake

**Koshi-an**—azuki bean paste

**Liliko'i**—passionfruit

**Lomi**—to massage, rub, or crush ingredients with the fingers

**Long Rice**—translucent mung bean noodles

**Lū'au**—young tops of taro plants; also, a Hawaiian feast

**Lumpia Wrappers**—wrappers used to make Filipino spring rolls

**Lychee**—small round fruit with sweet white flesh

**Mahimahi**—dolphinfish

**Mandoo Wrappers**—Japanese gyoza or Chinese wonton wrappers

**Marungay Leaves**—leaves with a citrus-like and slightly bitter flavor, used in Filipino cuisine

**Masago**—fish roe

**Mascarpone Cheese**—mild Italian cream cheese

**Mirin**—sweet rice wine

**Miso**—fermented soybean paste

**Mizuna**—Japanese cabbage

**Mochi**—steamed or pounded rice cake

**Mochiko**—glutinous rice flour

**Mung Bean Sprouts**—bean sprouts often used in Asian cuisine

**Musubi**—rice ball

**Nam Pla**—Thai fish sauce

**Namasu**—Japanese salad typically made with pickled carrots, daikon, and vinegar marinade

**Nori**—dried seaweed sheets

**Nuoc Mam**—Vietnamese fish sauce

**ʻŌhelo Berries**—rare berry grown in the uplands of Hawaiʻi

**Ogo**—red stringy seaweed

**Oyster Sauce**—oyster-flavored sauce

**Panko**—Japanese bread crumbs

**Patis**—Filipino fish sauce

**Peaberry Coffee Beans**—a type of pea-shaped coffee bean

**Pigeon Peas**—peas often used in canning

**Pipikaula**—dried beef jerky

**Plum Sauce**—sweet and sour condiment used in Chinese cooking

**Poi**—steamed, mashed, and fermented taro

**Poke**—cut-up pieces of raw fish with seasonings

**Ponzu Sauce**—tart, citrus-based sauce

**Portuguese Sausage**—cured, seasoned pork sausage

**Saimin**—unique Hawaiian soup made of wheat egg noodles

**Sake**—Japanese rice wine

**Sanbaizuke**—vegetables pickled in vinegar, soy sauce, and sugar

**Sate or Satay**—small pieces of grilled or barbecued meat, often served on a stick and eaten with a spiced sauce

**Shichimi Togarashi**—Japanese red pepper mix

**Shiofuku Kombu**—dried salted seaweed

**Shoyu**—Japanese soy sauce

**Somen Noodles**—fine noodles made from wheat flour

**Somen Tsuyu or Sauce**—sauce used with Japanese-style fine wheat flour noodles

**Sultana Raisins**—sweet raisins made from dried ripe sultana (or other) grapes

**Sushi**—Japanese vinegar-flavored rice

**Sweet Mochi**—Rice glutinous rice cake

**Takuan**—pickled turnip

**Taro**—edible corm of the taro plant; staple in Hawaiian cuisine

**Tempura**—battered and deep-fried seafood or vegetables

**Teriyaki**—soy-flavored sauce, used as a basting for grilled food

**Thai Sweet Chili Sauce**—condiment used in Thai cuisine

**Tī Leaf**—broad leaf of a tī plant

**Tilapia**—mild-flavored freshwater fish

**Tobiko**—fish roe

**Tofu**—fresh soybean curd or cake

**Togan**—Chinese winter melon

**Tripe**—stomach lining of a cow

**Tsubushi-an**—coarsely mashed azuki bean paste

**ʻUlu**—breadfruit

**Warabi**—Japanese term for fiddlehead fern shoots (the Hawaiian name is Hōʻiʻo; the Filipino name is paku)

**Wasabi**—horseradish, sold in paste or powdered form

**Won Bok Cabbage**—a type of Chinese cabbage

# RECIPE INDEX

# INDEX

# THANKS TO KTA STORES

**THANKS TO KTA SUPER STORES** for helping *What the Big Island Likes to Eat* come to fruition and supporting local farmers and food producers. Many of the food products used in the recipes can be bought at any of the five KTA stores.

KTA was founded by an immigrant from Hiroshima, Japan, seeking a better life in Hawai'i. After working for S. Hata, Koichi Taniguchi and his wife Taniyo, started a small grocery store in 1916 on the ground floor of a two-story building in Waiakea. In that small building, they raised nine children while running the store. In 1939 they opened a second store in downtown Hilo, and after the 1946 tsunami damaged the Waiakea store, they moved the entire operation to Hilo.

They kept expanding, opening stores in Kailua-Kona (1959), Puainako (1966), Keauhou (1984), and Waimea (1989). Their children, grandchildren, and great grandchildren succeeded them in the business and are still active in management. Today, KTA employs over 700 workers.

# ABOUT THE AUTHOR

Audrey Wilson is a food columnist, cooking instructor, and is the author of two locally-published cookbooks: *A Mother's Gift to Her Three Sons* (2007) and *An Eruption of Recipes from Volcano* (2002).

She writes a weekly column for the *Hawaii Tribune Herald* called "Let's Talk Food," and has taught cooking classes at Ke Anuenue Area Health Center, Hilo Adult Education, and several Big Island senior centers.

Wilson has traveled the world with her husband and has taken cooking classes in such places as: Paris, France; Sorrento, Italy; Florence, Italy; Chiang Mai, Thailand; Costa Brava, Spain; and New Orleans, Louisiana.

Wilson graduated from Hilo High School and received a BS in Home Economics from the University of Hawai'i at Mānoa. She and her husband, Jim Wilson, Publisher Emeritus of the *Hawaii Tribune Herald,* live in Volcano. There they preside over AJ's Volcano Cottage, a two unit bed and breakfast, and AJ's Volcano Cooking School.

# NOTES